The Rise of the Human Digital Brain: How Multidirectional Thinking is Changing the Way We Learn

The Rise of the Human Digital Brain: How Multidirectional Thinking is Changing the Way We Learn

By
Beatriz Pacheco

IAP
INFORMATION AGE PUBLISHING, INC.
Charlotte, NC • www.infoagepub.com

Library of Congress Cataloging-in-Publication Data

The CIP data for this book can be found on the LIbrary of Congress website (loc.gov).

Paperback: 978-1-64113-274-9
Hardcover: 978-1-64113-275-6
eBook: 978-1-64113-276-3

Printed in the United States of America

Cover design: Rebecca Jones

CONTENTS

DEDICATION

For Gilbert and Diego
The reasons for the journey
For Mom and Dad
Where the journey began

PREFACE

Most good ideas start with a child. I became an educator at the age of 23, but, to be honest with you, it was never the profession that I had dreamed of when I was growing up. I chose this profession because of a desire to be better at my most cherished role, the role of mother. I had no idea how much that one child would influence my life in so many positive ways.

My husband, who is now retired from the U.S. Army after serving 22 years, had an important job, and it was one that required that our family move almost every summer. As a result, I was often looking for a new job in the field of education, and I became a "jack of all trades." I started by teaching college freshman-level English courses to soldiers in Germany, and I eventually taught in New Mexico, Texas, North Carolina, South Korea, Oklahoma, and Kentucky. With each new move came the challenge of finding a job and gaining certifications. I worked at grade schools, middle schools, and high schools, and I have experience in public, private, and Department of Defense schools. I was constantly working, taking college courses, and being a mom and a wife.

What was initially a profession that I had never sought suddenly became one that I would not trade for the world. I met parents who, just like me, only wanted the best for their children. In every child's face, I began to see the hopes and dreams that each parent holds for his or her child. My purpose became clearer with each new position that I obtained.

The Rise of the Human Digital Brain:
How Multidirectional Thinking is Changing the Way We Learn, pages ix–x.

I noticed quickly that many of these children struggled with literacy skills. I had always been a good reader, but I really did not understand the complexities of reading until I directly encountered children who had such difficulty with comprehension. How could something that came so easily for me be such a struggle for them? I was constantly revising plans and looking for new ways to help my students. Then one day, I met a young man who put me on the road to a doctorate in the field of education. This young man came to my room every day before and after school for help (and sometimes just to chat). He tried so hard, but he really struggled with vocabulary and comprehension skills. No matter how hard he worked, he just could not quite grasp some of the concepts. I could not reconcile in my mind how someone who was so willing to work just could not get it. That was when I decided that if I was going to attempt to help change lives, I had to change mine first. I had to gain more knowledge.

The journey was not an easy one. I had a purpose, however. My purpose was to learn more so that I could help more children. There were barriers in my way, and without my husband and my son tutoring me in statistics and cheering me on, I would never have made it to the finish line. After I finally completed my doctorate, my husband told me that it would be a shame if all that knowledge only impacted a very limited number of children. He encouraged me to write down my ideas and methods and to share them with others in the hopes that new ideas of promoting literacy might spread. And so, this book, which would never have been written without my son and husband (the reasons for the journey), is about sharing ideas. It is about that young man who gave it everything he had every day in my class because he wanted to succeed. It is about all those teachers who look for new and innovative ways to educate young minds. And finally, it is about all the children sitting in classrooms across the world who are filled with potential and just waiting for someone to help them unlock it.

CHAPTER 1

THE TIME FOR EDUCATIONAL REFORM IS NOW

In his #1 *New York Times* bestseller *The Future of the Mind* (2014), popular theoretical physicist and futurist Michio Kaku states, "The introduction of MRI machines and a variety of advanced brain scans in the mid-1990s and 2000s has transformed neuroscience. We have learned more about the brain in the last fifteen years than in all prior human history, and the mind, once considered out of reach, is finally assuming center stage" (pp. 9–10).

This newly acquired information about the brain, its plasticity, and how we function as learners gives rise to the following question: what are we doing with this information to help advance educational outcomes? We now have the ability to create educational programs that are specifically designed to meet the needs of the individual, yet there is little indication that learning institutions are comprehensively incorporating this information into 21st century curriculum.

THE 21ST CENTURY MODEL OF EDUCATION

The apparent belief that the current system of education is "broken" is a common refrain amongst 21st century leaders outside of the field of education, but this belief does not sit well with those who have devoted their lives to educating and preparing the next generation. Many teachers, administrators, and educational

The Rise of the Human Digital Brain:
How Multidirectional Thinking is Changing the Way We Learn, pages 1–8.

leaders believe that there is enough existing evidence to support the claim that the current model is working, even if it is not a perfect model. Despite this belief, if you walk into any elementary, middle, or high school today, the teachers will probably tell you that their job is now harder than it was fifteen, ten, or even just five years ago. They might also tell you that this is due (at least in part) to changes in societal expectations, which include the expanse of technology in all settings. Many view the change itself as the problem and not the existing system. The prevailing belief is that we need to stop (or at least manage) the change rather than reimagining an entire system that has existed in the same form for over one-hundred and fifty years.

However, there are many barriers to successful system reform because the technological forces driving this change are not slowing down. This change is occurring so rapidly that by the time a total system reform is implemented, it may already be outdated as even-newer technology will already have emerged to replace existing technologies. The forces driving this historic change are already having such an impact on us that they are literally changing the way that we think and process information. Thus, returning to the "old way" of doing things is an impossibility.

I first began to recognize this change in 2012 when the high school where I worked as an English teacher began a one-to-one iPad initiative, which is an educational program where the district provides an iPad for each student to use either inside or outside of class or both. In this case, each student was issued an iPad for use both at home and at school. The introduction of this type of technology was new ground for educators across the country. The iPad, which Apple first introduced in 2010, came with no pre-existing instruction manual for how to proceed. The educators at my school were learning new processes right along with the students, and it was both exciting and frightening as the implications of this new tool for learning became evident.

After the iPads were distributed, the first thing that I noticed was the apprehension of seasoned educators regarding the use of this type of technology in the classroom. It was unfamiliar with new territory being chartered. We were on the frontier of a transformational period in education, and we were going to be given the opportunity to help write this new chapter in educational reform.

As I look back on that first year, I believe that the most interesting fact about the process was that, at the time, we had no idea what a huge impact technology would have on our students over the course of just five short years. The ubiquitous nature of the iPhone and now the iPad and the absence of information regarding the effects that this technology was having on the brain caused change to spread much more quickly than we could keep up with it. Our students were indeed changing faster than we could manage the change, and this led to some frustration along the way.

SOCIAL AND PHYSICAL TECHNOLOGIES

Because the educational system is a social construct, it adheres to what Thomas Friedman, author of *Thank You for Being Late* (2016), refers to as "social technologies." Friedman defines social technologies as "how we organize to capture the benefits of cooperation" (p. 200). Schools are meant to maximize our ability to cooperate in a global society. Technology offers us a new way to do that, and Friedman refers to these new ways as "physical technologies," which he defines as "innovations that make new social technologies possible" (p. 200). He references smartphones and how they make sharing ideas possible. Friedman also believes that physical technologies rely on social technologies. In other words, we must cooperate in order to maximize the benefits of our new technologies. These physical technologies are now so common that we have come to a point where we must teach students how to manage them in conjunction with their social technologies. This has created some unanticipated complications because we spend so much time trying to keep physical technologies out of classrooms that we risk interfering with our social technologies as well.

The term "digital citizenship" was created to explain how we should address these physical and social technologies in classrooms across the world. Digital citizenship is defined as the "norm of appropriate, responsible technology use" (Davidson, 2011, p. 17). As my school found after introducing the iPad to our students, this is something that must be explicitly taught. The Common Core Standards, which vary from state to state, have only recently realized the importance of addressing this need. These standards tend to remain focused on reinforcing stocks of information that are to be acquired during set periods of time. The current model of education, where everyone sits in rows and is delivered information based upon age rather than readiness, was not developed to address the needs of 21st century learners. The capabilities of 21st century technology were not something that could have been imagined when the model was originally adopted at the onset of the Industrial Age. We now have the ability to communicate in ways never before imagined, and the belief that the classroom is the main source of knowledge for students is a naïve one.

As new technologies are introduced into classrooms across the country, the changes that are occurring are not confined to modes of delivery of information. These changes are happening at a cellular level, and the very way that we process information is changing, yet the linear design of the curriculum (which will be more fully explained later in this chapter) has remained unchanged.

HISTORY OF THE 20TH CENTURY MODEL OF EDUCATION

The current model of education is based upon a linear design that favors the belief that there is an agreed upon body of knowledge that must be learned to achieve success. This model is the most common used in Western culture and is, therefore, the most widely recognized model for education globally. In this model, objectives are created, and methods are developed for the presentation of agreed upon content. Finally, a linear measure (or assessment) of acquired knowledge is conducted as proof of competence. The focus in this design is on teaching and how information should be delivered rather than on what type of knowledge it is hoped for the student to attain. The 21st century model still holds that the teacher has a "stock" of information and that this information should then "flow" to the student in one seamless process. What this model does not take into account is that the teacher is no longer the main source of information for 21st century students. Today's students are exposed to what Friedman refers to as "an acceleration of flows" of information from the internet and other readily available resources. Due to this acceleration of flows, students can now choose to measure what they are learning in the classroom against the knowledge that they discover on their own. As a result, a student's stock of knowledge is constantly changing as new flows form, and ideas are no longer static. This "democratization of knowledge" is obviously a far cry from how information was disseminated in past centuries.

The evolution of education. At the beginning of the 15th century, there were 30,000 unique, printed texts in all of Europe, and by the end of the century, there were roughly nine million. This exponential growth was the result of one great innovation: the printing press. At the time, the printing press posed a threat to educators in universities because they could not yet begin to envision how access to printed texts would revolutionize the way that education could be delivered and information could be disseminated (Goldstein & Otte, 2016). In order for these printed texts to be effective, educators had to focus on promoting mass literacy. As a result of the printing press, literacy became a benchmark of educational attainment and remains so to this day.

In 1800, James Pillans created the chalkboard by connecting small slate boards together to create a larger board that could be displayed at the front of the classroom, and it revolutionized the way that education could be delivered. Rather than having each student write on an individual slate board, the large board at the front of the room allowed the teacher to present ideas to the whole group at once. The teacher was now given a stage at the front of the classroom and was the focal point of all lessons. This idea spread quickly, and it helped to transform education and to streamline the delivery of information in the classroom.

There have been many changes since that time, and innovations introduced into classrooms over the last 40 years, such as whiteboards, projectors, personal computers, and tablet technologies, have all but replaced chalkboards in many educational settings in the 21st century. Despite the introduction of these innovations, standardized test scores for American students have remained flat over this same 40-year period. Although the introduction of technology into the classroom shows great promise, it has yet to demonstrate the type of growth that seems possible. This may be related to a variety of factors, some of which will be identified and discussed in more detail in future chapters.

One reason for the stagnant state of performance outcomes for students in the U.S. may be the fact that with each new innovation, the mode of delivery has changed very little. Since the introduction of the printed word and of the chalkboard, we have continued to expose students to the same linear modes of instruction. Education remains teacher centered, and little emphasis has been placed on individualizing education to maximize outcomes. We still imagine that we live in a world where the teacher is the main flow of information for students. We continue to rely on this linear system despite our knowledge that with the new physical technologies available to us, our social technologies should be changing as well. This necessary change is something that is not happening in most 21st century classrooms.

The emergence of the current model. The educational system developed in the United States was initially not governed by state or federal boards. In fact, most of its governance fell to parents. This began to change in the 1820s when the first functioning mechanized mill was established just outside of Boston, Massachusetts. Eventually, the town of Lowell, Massachusetts, became the biggest manufacturing center in North America. Demand for textiles increased, and a need for thousands of workers willing to work grueling twelve-hour shifts and six-day weeks grew. Many of these jobs were filled by girls and women. This was the dawn of the Industrial Revolution, and with it came a need for a new system of education that could help to train and prepare individuals to enter this new workforce. Because many of these new workers were female, the linear nature of the work fit well with their natural preference for linear processing. This need drove the changes in education that still exist to this day.

The Industrial Age, as it soon became known, introduced a new notion of control because of the impact of the machine. Just as technology is impacting the way that we process information today, machines impacted thinking in the 1800s. While living systems are able to control themselves, machines are controlled by operators. The first school systems were developed in the 1800s to adhere to the principles of a machine rather than a living organism. Control was transferred from the individuals to the operators, which in this case were the administrators, school boards, and teachers (Senge, Cambron-McCabe, Lucas, Smith et al., 2012).

Horace Mann, a Massachusetts state senator, quickly identified the newly emerging patterns, and he took action. In the early 1800s, public schools were called "common schools," and according to Mann, they were in desperate need of reform. He saw how new innovations in manufacturing were spreading quickly across the country, and he saw a need for this type of growth to occur in the school system as well. He quickly noticed that because only the poorest students had access to free education and all others had to pay tuition, many students were being lost to private schools. Mann teamed up with James Carter, who held a seat in the Massachusetts legislature and who also had experience running a private school.

Together, they devised a plan to take control of education from the parents and to place it under the control of state appointed experts and state trained teachers.

Mann formed the first state teacher college in the country in Lexington, Massachusetts, in 1822. He believed that a well-funded public education system could serve to transform society for the better. In 1837, Mann became the head of the first State Board of Education in the country. Thus began the government regulation of the public school system. Education became a process much like manufacturing. The goal was to produce an assembly line of students who could all perform at the same rate at the same time (Coulson, episode one, 2017). This system has held steady in structure and form, and it became the predominant model in the 20th century. Our current educational system is one that slowly evolved in order fit the needs of the Industrial Age.

THE 21ST CENTURY—THE NEED FOR A NEW MODEL

In the 21st century, there is a need to reimagine this system to fit what George Otte, the University Director of Academic Technology at the City University of New York (CUNY) Graduate Center, refers to as "the Age of the Internet" (Goldstein & Otte, 2016). Proposals to change the current model have met with little support or success. The "that's the way we've always done it" rationale seems to remain pervasive and, like unchecked kudzu (the climbing, coiling vines that quickly cover walls and buildings if not contained), it obscures our education system and cuts it off from desperately needed educational reforms. Many students still sit in single rows in classrooms that deliver (for the most part) the same material to a group of students primarily based upon age rather than on ability. This type of education is simply not viable in the 21st century.

What is linear thinking? Cathy Davidson, author of the 2011 book *Now You See It: How the Brain Science of Attention Will Transform the Way We Live, Work and Learn,* defines linear thinking as "a process of thought following known cycles or step-by-step progression where a response to a step must be elicited before another step is taken" (p. 15). A good linear thinker starts at step one and will strive to effectively complete that step before moving to step two. In short, linear thinking is recognized by its defined starting and end points. It is fragmented, and the relationship of the part to whole is supposed to be the end result. In this type of thinking, students learn that there is one right way to solve a problem rather than exploring all of the potential options. This type of learning caters more to the lower-order thinking skills of Bloom's Taxonomy such as knowledge (remembering) and comprehension (understanding), but it does not activate the higher order thinking skills of analysis, synthesis, and evaluation, all of which are necessary to develop critical thinking (Senge et al., 2012).

The Linear Model of Curriculum Development is derived from the education system that Mann set up in response to the manufacturing era model. In this model, information proceeds in a mainly sequential manner. Objectives are stated, learning experiences are selected and organized, and some type of evaluation occurs at the end of the delivery of the information. This curriculum is based upon the concept of linear thinking.

There was not a great deal of creativity required in order to work on an assembly line. School was designed (under Mann's model) to reinforce the type of thinking that would be necessary for the types of jobs that would be available for individuals in the workplace. These jobs were mostly industrial in nature.

In the 1940s, Ralph Tyler, education advisor to the White House under President Truman and President Eisenhower, formalized this linear form of curriculum when he developed the Tyler Model. This model, while not intended to reinforce a rigid type of instruction, did create a very systematic, four-step approach to teaching: determine objectives, identify educational experiences related to these objectives, organize these experiences, and evaluate the objectives. This model was also meant to help students tie learning to outside objectives. Tyler's hope was that learning would target students' beliefs, feelings, and emotions as well as their intellect. The Tyler Model is still considered by many to be the most effective model for curriculum development, and its introduction unwittingly provided females with a distinct advantage in the area of literacy attainment by reinforcing a linear model (Pinar, Reynolds, Slatter, &Taubman, 1995).

Other models of curriculum development. While Mann's vision of the linear model was progressive for its time, the limited understanding of the neurological underpinnings of the learning process inhibited the development of a system structured to meet the needs of the individual. This is also true of the Tyler Model, which has inhibited the introduction of spatial-mechanical and visual-graphic learning in the commonly accepted rigid, linear curriculum. We now have unprecedented access to technology, such as brain scans and MRI's, that allows us to see exactly how our brains process information, and we now know that technology is actually beginning to shape and change the very way that we think. Thanks to these advances in neuroscience, we have new insights that could help to shape the future of education throughout the world.

TECHNOLOGY AND THE DECLINE OF THE LINEAR MODEL

When I first started teaching students how to use the iPad as a tool for learning, I quickly found that the existing model needed to be expanded. Students no longer processed information in the traditional linear fashion that had been reinforced for over one-hundred and fifty years. They no longer needed to participate in rote processes aimed at helping them to memorize information and then to demonstrate knowledge of this information on matching or multiple-choice exams. These were students who could access information quickly. They could take that information and apply it to new situations. Things that were of interest to them, things that they really wanted to know about, were now available at the touch of a fingertip.

One good example of this is when my freshmen students were reading the story *Unbroken* about American World War II hero Louie Zamparini. The class was discussing the type of plane Zamparini flew, which was a B-24 called *The*

Green Hornet. The students were very interested in trying to visualize this type of plane. Before I knew it, one of my students accessed a link to the Dayton Air and Space Museum on his iPad, and he then used the mirroring feature of the device to project what was on his iPad to the screen at the front of the room so that it could be shared with the rest of the class. By accessing this link, we were able to take a virtual walk through the museum and actually see what a B-24 looked like. We were also able to see other World War II planes.

The lesson plan took a definite turn, but the students were much more engaged because the learning was now student-directed and not teacher-directed. True learning takes place when students are actively engaged in the process rather than being mindlessly directed towards a pre-determined goal. This is just one good example of how education can be a dynamic and engaging process, and technology can enhance this process by allowing students to take control of their own learning. In order to reinforce this type of learning, new models must be envisioned. If those new models are student-centered, the possibilities seem limitless.

CHAPTER 2

21ST CENTURY EDUCATION

How We Teach and Assess

In order to leverage the types of technological advances that are rapidly occurring in the 21st century, one area that we must focus on is how we train educators. Educators must now be prepared to effectively use technology in the classroom with the aim of advancing student outcomes.

We must also be willing to take a hard look at how we assess for college readiness. The type of standardized measures currently used may no longer be capable of accurately determining success in a workplace that will be dominated by constantly evolving technology. Because this technology is evolving so quickly, it will probably not exist in the same form from the time a student enters college to the time that he leaves it, yet the assessments used to measure college readiness, as well as the grading system used by most schools, remain stagnant.

STANDARDIZED ASSESSMENT

Daniel Koretz, author of *Measuring Up: What Educational Testing Really Tells Us* (2008), suggests that before questions for a standardized test can be created, there is a need to specify what knowledge and skills we want to measure. Therefore, if we want to measure college readiness, we need to determine which skills will be necessary for success in college. However, in the 21st century, the skills

The Rise of the Human Digital Brain:
How Multidirectional Thinking is Changing the Way We Learn, pages 9–26.

that will be assessed are being determined by people who literally think differently than those who will be entering college. That is why those who were educated prior to the introduction of technology into the classroom need to retrain their brains to understand how this new generation of technology savvy students learns.

Dr. Michael Merzenich, a driving force in the field of neuroplasticity, uses the term "competitive plasticity" as a way to explain this phenomenon. Competitive plasticity in adults is established when what is done over and over again assumes center stage in the brain, and as a result, new skills and patterns become harder to form unless focused attention is applied over a set period of time (Doidge, 2007). Once adulthood is reached, it becomes more difficult to create new patterns that will result in lasting change. For true change to occur, the individual has to be willing to acknowledge the differences between the established patterns and the new patterns, and he has to be willing to let go of old processes in order to learn new ones. Most colleges have yet to change the way that they deliver instruction because instructors prefer to teach using patterns with which they are comfortable. As a result, entering students are still being held to archaic standards of measurement (Davidson, 2011). This is why we continue to see books written that demonize technology and propagate the belief that it is the reason for the decline in proficiency scores. While this belief is not entirely untrue, it is only a part of the story.

In reality, there are multiple causes for this decline. When educational outcomes are measured using an assessment such as the ACT, whose function is to determine college readiness by measuring what a student already knows, the new flows of information available as a result of the introduction of technology are not being taken into consideration. The statistics that we rely upon regarding educational outcomes for students are based on assessments (such as the ACT) designed as traditional linear measures, but these assessments may no longer be adequate predictors of future success. For example, ACT composite scores reached a high of 21.1 in 2012, but this was followed by a steady decline. By 2016, the average ACT composite score was a 20.8 (Jaschik, 2016). While this is not a large decline by any means, it does demonstrate a lack of progress. Numbers should be going up, particularly because we have greater exposure to new flows of information due to the ubiquitous nature of technology in our world today.

When asked to quantify this decline, ACT attributed it to the number of students who took the test in each of the years cited. In 2012, 52% of high school seniors took the test, and in 2016, that percentage was up to 64% (Jaschik, 2016). This response only creates further questions regarding the inequity of opportunities provided to test takers from various backgrounds. If the number of students taking the test is increasing, and each of these students is presumed to have been provided with equal access to the information presented in these tests (as a result of Common Core Standards), shouldn't the numbers be going up and not down?

Another common assessment designed to predict potential college success is the SAT. The SAT is a test that was originally designed in 1926 to measure aptitude. This differed from the ACT because the SAT was designed to measure talents that might indicate possible future achievement. For example, one of the SAT's initial purposes was to identify students who might exhibit potential talent yet came from underprivileged backgrounds. It was not originally designed to simply measure what a student learned in school as the ACT was. With modern neuroscience exhibiting to us that there is such a thing as brain plasticity, a test developed mainly to measure innate ability is less of a predictor of future academic success than grades, which can be attributed to factors other than just innate ability (Strauss, 2014). College Board, the administrators of the SAT, PSAT, and AP exams, recognize this, and the SAT of today is no longer designed to measure innate ability. Rather, it is used to measure developed reasoning, or skills that are not only developed in school but are developed outside of school as well. While both SAT and ACT are attempting to change their focus to remain relevant, there are still many flaws in this system of measurement to predict future success.

In a 2017 *New York Times* article entitled "How to Take the SAT Like a Rich Kid," the author, an economically disadvantaged Hispanic student named Dylan Hernandez from Flint, Michigan, recounts how he found out about the preparation that students with greater access to resources as a result of higher economic status are able to take advantage of before taking a test such as the ACT or the SAT. Hernandez was fortunate enough to be granted a summer scholarship to attend the Phillips Exeter Academy's summer semester in New England. While there, he saw first-hand how many of these students, whose parents could afford the $10,000 price tag, were busy taking preparation courses for the SAT during the summer. This was a foreign concept to Hernandez, and it was an eye-opening experience for him as well. Hernandez was able to understand that the economic divide would indeed have an impact on his ability to go to college or to get a scholarship. So if we think again about the decline in recent ACT composite scores, and we are willing to agree with ACT's explanation that ACT test scores are going down because more students are taking the test, then we must also acknowledge that many of those who were taking the test in 2012 and before probably also had greater access to preparation.

To address the concern of equal access, College Board has recently partnered with Khan Academy, a free tutorial site that offers YouTube video lessons in a variety of core subjects, to personalize SAT preparation for students. SAT is now offering this free preparation based on PSAT scores. The PSAT is a preliminary SAT test that targets 10th and 11th grade students and also serves as a National Merit Scholarship Qualifying test. Once a student takes the PSAT and receives her scores, she is provided with access to a customized lesson that will help her to improve in areas of weakness identified by the test. This is certainly a step in the right direction, and it offers a way to bridge the "test-prep for a price" gulf that exists between the privileged and those who lack access to certain resources, but it still fails to acknowledge the root of the problem.

What our current system has yet to address is the fact that tests such as the ACT and the SAT may no longer serve as adequate measures of the type of learning that is taking place for 21st century students. Today's students do not learn in the traditional linear models that have been reinforced by school systems for more than a century. While ACT and SAT preparation courses can help a student to memorize information and learn how to navigate certain types of questions, they do not always accurately reflect what 21st century students really know or need to know. They also do not measure spatial-mechanical reasoning skills, yet this is area where boys typically excel.

STANDARD GRADING SCALES

In the 1950s, Benjamin Bloom, an American educational psychologist, established a way to assist educators in classifying educational learning objectives into levels of complexity and specificity. To do this, Bloom developed three hierarchical models used to classify these objectives. The learning objectives in the cognitive domain are the most well-known by educators, and they are comprised of the following domains: knowledge, comprehension, application (which are considered lower-order thinking skills), analysis, synthesis, and evaluation (which are considered higher-order thinking skills). Learning objectives, assessments, and activities are often developed around these cognitive domains. Many educators today design instruction and assessment around the lower-order thinking skills of knowledge, comprehension, and application because these skills are more concrete and easier to assess.

In her book *Now You See It: How the Brain Science of Attention Will Transform the Way We Live, Work, and Learn* (2011), Cathy Davidson reminds us that if we want our schools to work differently, we need to develop new metrics of assessment. The type of assessment used in most schools today is based upon a linear numerical and letter scale that measures mostly lower-order thinking skills. The concept of assigning quantitative grades, according to Davidson, may have originated in the late 1800s when numerical and letter grades were used at Cambridge University to accompany written comments. This type of assessment was developed prior to the development of Bloom's hierarchical model, but it did tend to focus on what Bloom would later describe as "lower-order thinking skills," and it was not initially recommended as a reliable means of evaluation for the higher-order thinking skills that would later be identified by Bloom's model.

By 1914, Frederick J. Kelly, who wrote his doctoral dissertation on variability and standardization, developed a scale that would eliminate subjective judgement in the marking of papers. Kelly developed the Kansas Silent Reading Test to create an objective measure of learning goals. He devised questions that had no ambiguity; therefore, each multiple-choice question had only one correct answer. An unfortunate consequence of this type of testing was that it focused mainly on the lower-order thinking skills, where essays focused more on "relationships, connections, structures, organization, and logic" (Davidson, 2011, p. 115).

As we consider the type of learning that is occurring in 21st century classrooms, where information that previously had to be memorized is now just a finger tap away, it seems that this type of antiquated form of assessment would have run its course. Unfortunately, this type of testing still remains standard in schools across the United States and around the world today. If our goal in "the Age of the Internet" is to move students to the center of their own learning, then we must envision and implement new tools as well as new models to maximize learning outputs.

TECHNOLOGY AND EDUCATION

One way that has been used to address the changes occurring in 21st century students is the introduction of more modern technology into the learning environment. One such modern form of technology that school systems favor is the iPad. According to Apple Press, in 2012 more than 1.5 million iPads were deployed in classrooms across the United States, and the iPad is one of the fastest growing forms of technology being introduced in many classrooms today (Reid, Strnadová, & Cumming, 2013). As of 2014, nearly one in three public and private school students in the United States were using the iPad, a touch screen tablet first introduced by Apple in 2010, for educational purposes (Herold, 2014). The iPad is unique because it has the capability of running third party "apps," which are applications provided by vendors other than the manufacturer of the device (Christensson, 2011). These apps provide students with a variety of multi-sensory learning opportunities, and educators around the world are beginning to recognize the iPad's potential use as an instructional tool.

The iPad, with its multimodal (kinesthetic, auditory, and visual) and multidirectional (with no fixed starting point) functions, certainly appears to have the potential to impact learning for millions of students. Additionally, the various apps that are easily accessible via the iPad make it a novel way for instructors to present information. When the iPad is used for literacy instruction, it appears that the multimodalities inherent in the device would make it possible to positively impact vocabulary and comprehension skills for adolescents identified as "low-achieving readers." According to a 2000 study by the National Reading Panel, such readers are those identified as "older children with poor reading progress, varying in intelligence, at least some of whom achieve poorly in other academic areas" (p. 90). This is a population that is currently underserved. These are the students who made it through grade school without mastering the basic, surface-level reading skills necessary to build true comprehension. Currently, the needs of this population are not adequately addressed, and many leave school feeling that college is not a possibility because of something as simple as lack of adequate decoding skills that technology could easily help them to mitigate (National Reading Panel, 2000).

In Neil Selwyn's 2016 book entitled *Is Technology Good for Education?,* he notes that there is little evidence available to support the sustained improvement of teaching and learning as a result of the introduction of the iPad into the educational setting. As I reviewed data for the study presented in this book, I found this to be the case. Many literacy programs touted as effective means of addressing literacy deficits were found to have either no or very limited impact on outcomes. For example, Alan Cheung and Robert Slavin (2014) conducted a review of the effects of technology applications on reading outcomes for struggling readers. This was a meta-analysis that focused on a total of 20 studies focused on approximately 7,000 students who were determined to be struggling readers in grades one through six. The study measured the results of the following technology applications: the Lindamood Phonemene Sequence Program; Read, Write, & Type; *Fast ForWord*; and other supplemental CAI (computer assisted instruction) programs. The studies indicated that Read, Write, & Type and the Lindamood Phoneme Sequence Program produced the largest effect size, but overall, educational technology produced a rather small but positive effect on struggling readers' comprehension and fluency. A small effect size would equate to what would normally be expected during one year of education (Hattie, 2012). What this means is that these programs did very little to advance learning beyond what would typically be expected in one year of classroom exposure. So if technology in itself is not the answer to our educational woes, what is?

INTERACTION CURRICULUM MODEL

Hilda Taba and Paul Cohen developed The Interaction Curriculum Model, also known as the Dynamic Model, in the 1960s in an attempt to introduce a less structured, less linear model for curriculum development. Its purpose was to improve upon Tyler's Model and to address its weaknesses. The Interaction Model is made up of objectives, methods, evaluations, and contents. Figure 2.1 demonstrates the nonlinear nature of this model:

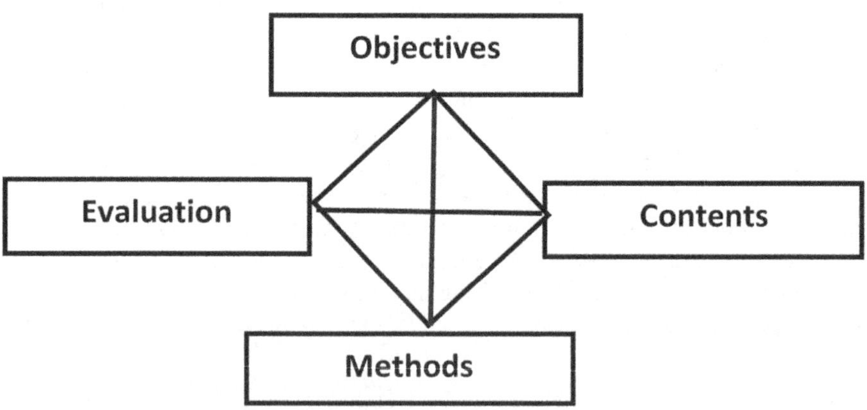

FIGURE 2.1. Taba's Interaction Model (Brady, 1995, p. 81)

The four elements are not considered linear; rather, they are considered interactive and modifiable. In other words, they are subject to change as needs arise. Additionally, a change to one of the elements will cause changes to other elements, which makes it a very dynamic model. For example, an evaluation of prior knowledge could precede an introduction of objectives. This could have a positive impact on learning because the starting point is determined by student knowledge rather than randomly determined by a curriculum that assumes that all students have access to the same prior knowledge. This is important because each individual is unique, and we build a repertoire of skills that are unique to our time in human history. At this point in history, we are moving away from fixed patterns of thought and into more multidirectional patterns because of the impact of technology on the brain. This model is not fixed like the linear model, and it certainly is a better fit for the learning needs of students who are morphing from linear thinkers to multi-directional thinkers.

The new modes of learning available via the multimodalities of technology such as the iPad are designed to help students focus on outcomes rather than solely on subject matter. Instead of simply summarizing information provided in a textbook, students can now demonstrate learning through a variety of modes after analyzing and synthesizing information that may come from a variety of sources. Teachers become resources rather than fountains of knowledge. The educator is also transformed from being the main source of information to a support resource whose primary mission is to guide the nonlinear learning experience, thus reinforcing the model. In other words, the new job of the educator is to direct learning for each student rather than to impart knowledge to the masses.

The availability of new modes of learning allows instructors to use descriptive analytics, which is basic information about a student that may be used to identify his unique learning behaviors. This means that we may now use descriptive data to determine a student's prior exposure to information and to learn specific demographic information that may help the instructor to create an individualized lesson plan for each student (Goldstein & Otte, 2016).

Technology also allows us to use predictive analytics to predict success or failure. We can use the data that is compiled to determine if a student is keeping up with the reading, comprehending what he read, and developing the skills necessary for success (Goldstein & Otte, 2016). Rather than having to wait for a teacher to analyze and grade hundreds of quizzes or essays, the information gathered through new advances in technology can provide instant feedback so that less of the instructor's time is spent on evaluation and more is spent on the creation of educationally sound practices designed to fit the needs of each individual student. This model supposes that the instructor is going to use this time effectively. Teachers have, by practice, become so indoctrinated into a system that values teaching to a set curriculum that they often forget to stop and reassess teaching practices when a student fails. Frustration by both the teacher and the student is often the result.

Technology-enhanced learning may be a good support for instruction delivered in the classroom, but it should be viewed as just that—a support. If we envision technology as a replacement for educators in the classroom, then we risk losing the type of critical, deep-level thinking that can be encouraged through active engagement and questioning. By introducing a new curriculum model, such as the Dynamic Model, into the classroom, students can take greater control of their own learning and educators can take their places as facilitators of complex processes.

If the educator takes time to introduce the four key elements of the model and then allows the student to select a starting place, the outcomes might be better. However, the teacher must still be there to direct students as they encounter stumbling blocks. The students will not be ready to direct their own exploration of information until they have a firm understanding of how to use the critical-thinking skills of analysis and synthesis. They will not learn these skills by merely googling information. They must be explicitly taught how to be discerning in the information that they choose to believe, and they must understand how to analyze that information effectively. The ability to synthesize newly learned information could prove to be an area where technology may provide strong gains. Once students have learned a process, analyzed information, and determined its importance, they are then free to apply this information to new concepts. And they have already been taught how to think for themselves!

This type of learning will reinforce the connection between our physical technologies (iPads, smart phones, etc.) and our social technologies (how we organize and capture the benefits of cooperation through the social systems that we have in place) to help us speed up our evolution. As it stands, our physical technologies are far more advanced than our social technologies. Our brains are not equipped to keep up with such rapid changes, and we have difficulty managing our physical technologies as a result (Friedman, 2016). As renowned child psychologist Jean Piaget stated in his theory of cognitive development, we are now in a constant state of "cognitive disequilibrium" where there is too much information and too little time for our brains to adjust to this overload. This is due to so many things accelerating at once that we are in a perpetual struggle to keep up. It is up to us to restore equilibrium by continuously adjusting our understanding of the world. We must become more adept at predicting the challenges that are ahead and responding rapidly. We can no longer just wait for things to fall apart before we address them. We must be forward thinkers who look to the future with a keener and more discerning eye. If we can teach our children how to do this, they will indeed become 21st century learners.

TEACHER TRAINING

Adequate teacher training is one important component lacking in our current system of education. There are two levels of training that need to be addressed if outcomes are to improve: 1) the neurological aspects of the learning process, and 2) how language and literacy skills are developed.

First, educators must obtain at least a general understanding of the neurological underpinnings of the learning process. Because of modern advances in neuroscience, we know more about the brain, to include how human brains can demonstrate gender differences, and this information can be critical when it comes to developing learning models. For example, most males prefer learning that is spatial-mechanical in nature. They learn by doing, and they are kinesthetic by nature. At the 2017 National Conference on Innovative Teaching Strategies, Dr. Michael Gurian, noted expert on gender differences and their impact on learning, shared the theory that this learning preference is a direct result of the amount of testosterone the fetus is exposed to in the womb. According to Dr. Gurian, to effectively teach males in the classroom, teachers need to be aware of this learning preference that affects about 80% of male students. In contrast, most females are more language-based learners, and they can effectively learn in linear patterns and by lecture. More information regarding these learning preferences will be covered in later sections of this book, but these are important differences that are all too often ignored.

Additionally, the length of time that it takes for a human brain to mature is about twenty-five years. One of the most crucial periods in this development is during adolescence when the type of neural reorganization that can dramatically impact development is occurring. After puberty, the prefrontal cortex develops new cells, and new synapses are formed. As these new synapses (or connections) are created, a decade of pruning also occurs. Weaker connections are removed while stronger connections are reinforced (Eagleman, 2015). What is repeated through practice will become ingrained while what is not repeated will become obsolete. Because adolescence is a time of tremendous cognitive change, a better understanding of these changes could be leveraged by educators to provide learning opportunities that will lead to stronger growth in important skills. One of these skills is literacy.

To effectively teach literacy skills, knowledge of how the brain develops the patterns necessary to support reading is a must. Teachers should develop an understanding of peak periods of brain development and what can happen when learning is interrupted during these periods. For example, we know that there are areas of white matter in the brain that are critical to reading development. The act of reading can be divided into phonological (auditory) and orthographic (visual) processing. Different neural pathways are used for each, and the development of these pathways influences literacy development (Yeatman, Dougherty, Ben-Shachar, & Wandell, 2012). Because the peak period for the development of these pathways is between kindergarten and third-grade, this is the time when reading skills should be reinforced, and it is also when reading disabilities, such as dyslexia, may become apparent. If a learning disability is caught within this crucial period, there is an opportunity to mitigate the impact of the disability (James, 2015).

It is also crucial to understand how the brain develops the mechanisms that will support literacy skills. For example, understanding the difference between constrained and unconstrained reading skills is an important first step in this process. As students are taught to read, much time is focused on the constrained reading skills of phonemic awareness and letter recognition, which are limited in scope and number because there are only so many letters and sounds that need to be learned for decoding to occur. Unconstrained reading skills, which are limited in scope and consist of components such as vocabulary knowledge and critical thinking, are not given as much attention. This can have an impact on young students in the early stages of reading development because the deep-level reading strategies that lead to comprehension should be just as important as the surface-level reading strategies of decoding and phonemic awareness.

The way that basic decoding skills are taught is also important. The use of synthetic phonics for reading instruction relies upon the synthesis of letters and sounds to construct meaning, so it is more auditory in nature. It takes less time for the brain to process auditory data than it takes for it to process visual data, which requires more complex processing. Because we are aware that our senses work in concert with one another to interpret our reality, it is also important to note that although we process auditory data more quickly than visual data, it does not appear that way to us in real time. If you clap your hands in front of you, you will see your hands meet and hear the clap at the same time, but in reality, the sound precedes the sight of your hands meeting together. This is because each type of sensory information takes a different amount of time to process, but the brain collects the information and processes it in such a way that our conscious awareness lags behind the physical world (Eagleman, 2015).

The use of analytic phonics, which is "a more accelerated form of phonics where children are taught to recognize whole words by sight and later to break the word into smaller units of sound" (Johnston, Logan, & Watson, 2009, p. 176), incorporates both senses, but it begins with visual processing and then moves to auditory processing. This information may be helpful to teachers who want to leverage the way that the brain processes information when developing lessons that will heighten awareness and fit with desired objectives.

When decoding is the focus of a literacy lesson, it is important to note that male students will often do better when synthetic phonics are used to teach decoding skills. This is because of the differences in the way a male brain processes language as compared to a female brain.

DIFFERENCES IN HOW MALES AND FEMALES LEARN

Dr. Michael Gurian, bestselling author, researcher, and speaker who is known for his ability to combine scientific research with people's everyday lives, explains that the 21st century model of education is skewed towards the learning needs of the female mind. He notes that the school system as it exists today is not boy friendly. This may have been the unintentional result of creating a system with a goal of producing factory workers who would need to be linear in thought. As noted earlier, many of the factory workers in the textile mills that originated in

Massachusetts were female. Massachusetts was also where the first teachers' college originated, so the system may have unintentionally been created to meet the learning styles of females to meet the demands of this emerging workforce. To understand this more thoroughly, it is important to know the primary differences between the male and female brain and how these differences affect cognition.

Dr. Gurian notes that all brains start out as female, and levels of testosterone peak at about four months; by six months, the male and female brains have been set up in utero. Lower levels of testosterone are associated with better verbal skills, and higher levels of testosterone are associated with stronger visual-spatial skills, which are associated with our ability to tell where objects are in space. Because most females are more adept with verbal skills, this can be associated with lower levels of testosterone in utero (Gurian, 2017a). Scientists have been able to identify at least 100 gender differences in the brains of male and female fetuses at 26 weeks of pregnancy, and many of these unique differences will remain throughout life. Part of these differences may be found in the central nervous system, which contains both gray and white matter. Male brains demonstrate 6.5 times more gray matter activity in areas of the brain related to intelligence and female brains demonstrate approximately 9.5 times more white matter activity in areas of the brain related to intelligence (Gurian, 2017a; James, 2015).

The gray matter in our brains is located mainly on the surface of the brain. Gray matter areas of the brain are also localized and work as information and action-processing centers. In other words, gray matter serves to translate all the sensory information that the body receives into chemical data that the brain's synapses can then interpret. Because boys' brains demonstrate more gray matter connections in areas related to intelligence, which are primarily associated with processing and cognition, most boys are more kinesthetic and more adept at visual, mechanical, and spatial skills (such as parallel parking). This can also lead boys to develop "tunnel vision" when they become engrossed in a task or a game (Gurian, 2017a; Jantz, 2014).

Girls, on the other hand, have more white matter connections that are related to intellectual skills. White matter is mainly comprised of myelinated nerve fibers called axons, and these axons coordinate communication between different brain regions. Thus, girls are often better at connecting thoughts and words, and they are more verbal than boys (Gurian, 2017a; James, 2015;). White matter activity is also associated with literacy because learning to read is a complex process that requires active coordination between several areas of the brain.

Learning to read requires coordinated development of key white matter pathways, and these generally see their greatest development between kindergarten and 3rd grade and will stabilize before middle school. The brain matures in a sequential manner, and some circuits tend to develop and stabilize while others remain capable of plasticity. Failure to fully develop the pathways necessary for literacy development can lead to struggles with literacy skills into adolescence and adulthood. Additionally, girls use both the left and right hemispheres of the brain to process language. Most males have verbal centers in only the left hemisphere, and this gives girls an advantage over boys in verbal processing. Our current system of education is based mostly on a verbal-literacy platform, which poses a disadvantage to males and provides an advantage to females (Gurian, 2017b).

In addition, the verbal-literacy platform preferred by most schools coupled with the fact that spatial intelligence is rarely measured or valued gives females another advantage. It has been established that boys will have stronger visual-spatial and mechanical-reasoning skills than verbal skills, yet their area of strength is often not measured in traditional educational settings.

One of the reasons that boys tend to like video games more than girls do is that video games are highly spatial-mechanical and rich in visual graphics, so they stimulate the right side of the brain, which is devoted to mechanical reasoning (Gurian, 2017a). This can provide both an advantage as well as a disadvantage for boys. On the plus side, boys will remain very focused on their objective and their tenacity will often result in the development of new strategies. When something is of interest to a boy, he will often not stop until he masters a concept. On the negative side, video games are highly addictive, and this comes at a cost. The need for the constant rush that occurs as dopamine is released when (for example) new levels of a game are mastered can lead to lack of sleep, loss of focus on important tasks, and a high release of stress hormones when the game is removed. In terms of the school setting, if a boy is too focused on thinking about when he will have more time to play his game, he will not be focused on the lesson being taught in the classroom. This can also have a significant impact on homework as many boys choose to use their time at home to play games, and homework is of little importance, so minimal effort will be exerted.

One other notable difference between the male brain and the female brain is that the human memory center known as the hippocampus is often larger in females, and this allows females to revisit emotional situations more than boys do. This too can have both a negative and a positive impact on girls. A larger hippocampus may cause girls to get stuck in a loop of rumination if under stress, and this can have a negative impact on processing (Gurian, 2017b). However, the hippocampus is also necessary for the brain to lay down memories that are crucial for both language and reading development, and this gives females an advantage in these areas.

Dr. Gurian also refers to the "bridge brain" that exists in one in five males and females. This type of brain is a bi-gender brain that contains nearly equal qualities of male and female brains. These brains are hardwired towards the middle of the gender-brain spectrum. As a result, male "bridge brains" are often more adept at verbal skills, yet they are equally adept at visual-spatial and mechanical reasoning skills (Gurian, 2017).

The left side of the brain, which is where the analytical, logical, and verbal skills are primarily distributed, processes information in a linear manner. This means that it goes from part to whole as it analyzes and learns new processes.

The right brain tends to see the whole picture first and not the details. This is a crucial difference in thinking. Because we know that girls are capable of processing language in both hemispheres of the brain, we can assume that their thinking processes may be more linear than those of boys, who are mostly oriented towards the right hemisphere of the brain. Girls also have more emotive connections and fewer visual-spatial centers in the brain (Gurian, 2017b; James, 2015). As we look at the model that has emerged in the current U.S. school system, it is indeed a linear one, and it meets the learning needs of one group more than the other.

How do all these cognitive differences translate into educational performance? As noted earlier, girls traditionally fall three points below boys on achievement tests in math and science. However, boys fall ten points below girls in literacy skills (Gurian, 2017b). There is a gap in both cases, but the literacy gap is wider and will be more difficult to close as a result. When conducting my study regarding boys and literacy skills both with and without the aid of technology, my hope was that the kinesthetic and multisensory nature of the iPad would lead to greater gains in vocabulary and comprehension for boys, thus making some progress in closing the literacy gap between boys and girls.

FEMALES AND TECHNOLOGY

Girls can benefit from the multidirectional modes of learning available via tablet technologies, but they must tap into their verbal skills to do so. As a female researcher working on a dissertation between 2014 and 2017, I found myself comparing the old modes of learning I was introduced to in the 1980s to the new modes I was using in this new era of technology. I used to spend hours in the library pouring over books and articles to gather information to write papers. I would then go to a computer lab to use the computer for nothing more than word-processing services. While working on the literacy study presented in this book, I went to the library only once for a research-related question. I was able to use the online data bases that the university's library provided to research and compile information that was timely, and I also found myself using very multidirectional methods in my research and employing the multimodalities of the iPad by incorporating auditory, tactile, and visual strategies into my information gathering process. Additionally, my university provided access to librarians who were available for questions all days of the week via an online platform, and responses to questions were rapid and helpful.

I did not learn how to use my iPad in doctoral-level classes, however. Because I had the great fortune to work at a high school that was an early adopter of a one-to-one iPad technology model, I had to learn how to locate the best applications and features of the iPad for use in my own teaching. Thus, I became much more aware of its potential uses for educational purposes. I then transferred that knowledge to my own research, and I used applications such as Notability to take lecture notes and to record the instructor's voice while simultaneously typing my notes. When I went home, I was able to listen to the lecture again while reviewing my notes. I could also tap on any word in the typed notes, and it would jump to that exact place in the lecture.

When it came to research, I had a variety of ideas that I wanted to explore. I started with two main concepts: literacy and technology. From there, I decided not to take a primarily linear path to finding information. I did a broad search and jumped around from one area to another. I found many articles that I may have overlooked if I had taken the more traditional approach. I also found that there were very limited studies available regarding the use of the tablet based technology for literacy instruction. This was a gap in the research that I hoped to help fill with my study. Soon, I was able to connect the dots in a logical (and probably linear) fashion to determine a feasible direction for my study. It is important to note that while this linear process remained an important component of my research, it was not the only nor was it the primary method used as I researched.

As I conducted my research and found data to support the fact that our current education system tends to work in favor of the learning styles of females, I began to think about the impact that this should be having on the success of females in the workplace. According to a 2015 article published in the U.S. Education section of *Time Magazine*, 29.9% of men held a B.A. degree in 2015 and 30.2% of women held the same degree. However, in the age group of 25–34-year old individuals, 37.5% of women held B.A. degrees while 29.5% of men held this same degree (Feeney, 2015). Despite this increase in educational attainment for females, fewer positions of leadership are held by women, and there is still a noticeable wage gap between men and women. I realize that there are many reasons for this, but perhaps one key reason is that, despite the linear nature of education and the verbal platform that it relies upon to disseminate information, the workplace does not always prioritize these skills in leaders. Leaders in the workplace are often those who use divergent thinking. This type of thinking, often referred to as thinking "outside the box," is often valued, and this is something that boys tend to do more naturally than girls.

One good example of this is when I took a group of students, both males and females, to work on a project boxing supplies to send to a foreign country impacted by a hurricane. I watched the differences in the approaches of the females and the males when it came time to determine how to efficiently package the materials. The girls got to work immediately. They formed a line, and each girl picked up an empty box and then proceeded to go to each pile of materials, select the correct number of items, and then place them in a box until it was filled. Each girl would then get another box to start the process again. The boys, on the other hand, grouped together to discuss a strategy. They determined that they could work faster if they stationed one person who would count out the number of materials needed for each box at each of the piles. Each of the remaining boys would then pick up an empty box and, in no particular order, go to each pile and have the young man at that station fill the box. This was a less linear process. The funny part about this was that after the boys were finished with their meeting and started their process, the girls had nearly finished packing all their boxes.

At the time, I thought that it was just a rather humorous anecdote, but as I have learned more about the differences between how males and females think, this image returned to me, and it made more sense. Each group was doing what came naturally to them. I believe that there is value in both types of thinking, and perhaps the introduction of technology into educational settings can create a paradigm shift. Greater exposure to technology may help females to develop their visual-spatial skills and encourage them to think "outside the box." However, the linear nature of processes should not be lost as a result.

The key seems to be getting people to analyze and synthesis information when it will provide a substantial benefit in approaches to complex processes. Rote processes, such as packing materials in a box or memorizing facts, may not require so much analysis and synthesis to be effective. We know that the brain is capable of refining itself as it masters a wide repertoire of skills and abilities. Changes in synaptic construction can occur when certain actions are repeated over time. Therefore, what we pay attention to matters. This is an important fact to remember because what most of us tend to pay attention to in the 21st century is technology.

It is also important to recognize the emergence of the new way of thinking being reinforced by the introduction of technology into classrooms across the world. As we introduce multidirectional functions, we are also reinforcing multidirectional thinking, yet we still continue to follow the linear processes introduced into classrooms over one-hundred and fifty years ago. Worse yet, we still tend to rely on primarily linear measures such as the ACT and SAT to determine educational readiness.

A MULTIDIRECTIONAL APPROACH TO EDUCATION

According to Abigail Norfleet James, author of *Teaching the Male Brain: How Boys Think, Feel, and Learn in School* (2015), one group that stands to benefit tremendously from the emerging multimodal and multidirectional features that are an inherent part of today's digital literacy skills is adolescent males, who continue to lag behind their female counterparts in literacy skills. According to a 2011 report from the National Center for Educational Statistics, only 42% of 4th graders were at or above proficient level in reading (as cited in Cheung & Slavin, 2014). This problem is particularly evident in male students. Longitudinal data indicate that from 1990 to 2012, there was little change in literacy skill variances between male and female students.

This is also evidenced by the results from a 2012 report of the reading portion of the National Assessment of Educational Progress (NAEP), which indicates that at ages 9, 13, and 17, girls had an 11- to 12-point advantage over boys. In 2012, the same data showed that boys had made some progress, but mainly among 9-year-old children. Once the boys reached adolescence, there was little to no growth in literacy. During the same period, boys enjoyed a 3-point advantage over girls in mathematics (as cited in James, 2015). It is important to note that all these scores are the result of traditional, standardized measures. These statistics are being used because currently, they are the only data that exists to evidence the growth or decline of skills.

There are many studies supporting the theory that most boys demonstrate an ease with mechanical reasoning, skill with moving objects, and a preference for learning via technology. Studies regarding sensory differences between male and female adolescents indicate that most boys are kinesthetic learners and that math and science are often easier for boys because both disciplines lend themselves to hands-on learning. This preference for hands-on learning opportunities is an important learning style difference that should be considered when creating instruction for boys.

Because neuroscience indicates that *all* individuals learn best when a variety of senses are activated during the process of learning new information, the use of instructional tools such as the iPad may have the potential to positively affect learning outcomes: however, careful consideration must be given to how these instructional tools are implemented in the classroom so that the outcomes remain positive and do not impede learning processes (Gardner & Davis, 2013).

Because of the growing availability of multimodal opportunities in the classroom setting, it seems that boys should be making strong academic gains, but this has yet to be the case, and the reasons for this are not quite clear. Davidson (2011) noted that current linear forms of assessment employed in most school systems may not provide a true picture of what students actually know. Due to the rapid spread of technology in modern classrooms, multidirectional modes of instruction are being employed more than ever before. These multidirectional modes of instruction often do not match the linear means of assessment. Because the mode of instruction and means of assessment often do not match, the assessments may not be good indicators of whether students are being adequately prepared for the future. A good example of this is the teaching and assessment of vocabulary and comprehension skills. While concepts can easily be taught in classrooms today via tablets and other forms of technology, it is more difficult to measure skills of comprehension and vocabulary attainment using the same mode. This may result in inconsistent outcomes because when the assessment does not match the mode of instruction, the results may be questionable (Gardner & Davis, 2013).

To better understand the potential instructional impact of tablet technology such as the iPad in modern classrooms, the learning process itself must be considered. Jean Piaget explained that children learn through a layered process by first taking in new information and then adapting and applying that new knowledge to previously existing schemas, which are stores of existing knowledge used as frames of reference when learning new information. At certain stages of development, children may experience cognitive disequilibrium as they struggle to balance what they know with what they are learning. According to Piaget, cognitive disequilibrium occurs "when a child's existing schemas are not capable of explaining what it can perceive around it" (Piaget, 1962, as cited in Burnett, 2010, p. 145). Children will actively question during the stage of cognitive disequilibrium and then "expand their intelligence by balancing their cognitive understanding to achieve equilibrium" (as cited in Burnett, 2010, p. 146). The introduction of technology into the classroom for literacy instruction may allow children who experience cognitive disequilibrium to find new and innovative ways to expand existing schemas. The medium used for reading instruction will impact the way that the information is processed, and new information might be adapted and applied differently for each different medium (Wolf & Barzillai, 2009).

WHAT DOES THE RESEARCH SAY?

When we come across a new problem, we use conscious deliberation to attack the problem. According to David Eagleman, neuroscientist and author of *The Brain: The Story of You* (2015), when we practice new skills, they eventually sink below the level of consciousness and become "hardwired." We no longer must use conscious deliberation to complete the task, and we revert to procedural memory, which is a long-term memory that represents how to do things automatically (or with automaticity). This requires less cognitive effort and is both rapid and energy-efficient. Our brains will continue to rewire themselves throughout our lives, and what we practice the most will eventually become automatic, thus requiring less energy and becoming more efficient. What we are paying attention to and practicing daily in the 21st century nearly all centers around technology. This again reminds us that technology, if used effectively, should be a leverage point in the field of education, but we also need to pay attention to what is lost (or pruned) out of young developing minds when we make more room for the practice of technology.

Dr. Maryanne Wolf, director for the Center of Reading and Language Development at Tufts University, suggested that because people can physiologically read in multiple ways, what is learned and absorbed from what is read will be influenced by both the content of the reading and the medium that is used to read the information (Wolf & Barzillai, 2009). Traditional reading practices involve a very linear pattern of thought, and this encourages the reader to connect information sequentially in order to anticipate outcomes (Wolf, 2010). As the digital reading brain is a new phenomenon and does not follow the linear process of reading established over centuries, learners are in a state of cognitive disequilibrium where they must question the information provided in a way that is nonlinear. This creates challenges when connecting prior knowledge and formulating new ideas.

This new multidirectional model may also provide some advantages. Multidirectional thinking may lead to the exploration of previously untried methods to gain knowledge. As new patterns of thought emerge, new forms of learning are created. Lory Hough (2015) wrote an article about Harvard professor Todd Rose, who has studied the transition of education from an Industrial Age linear model to one that is more individualized. In this article, it was noted that if teachers can harness the capabilities of the iPad effectively, it is possible to couple these capabilities with current understanding of neuroscience and the emerging "science of the individual" to create an educational plan for students that does not rely on group averages.

CHAPTER 3

BRAIN-BASED LEARNING IN THE 21ST CENTURY

WHO BENEFITS FROM THE LINEAR MODEL?

There is a well-known achievement gap between males and females in the areas of math and science. Michael Gurian cites recent research indicating that the gap in math and science achievement between males and females is roughly three points with boys having the advantage. We are now racing to add STEM (science, technology, engineering, and math) to curriculum to lessen this gap for girls. What is not as well publicized is the fact that there is also a literacy gap between males and females. As noted in the previous chapter, females enjoy a ten-point lead over boys in literacy achievement, yet we are not as focused on creating programs to address this urgent concern.

We know that our current system of education (based on the 20th century model) uses a verbal-literacy platform that is very linear in nature. Because most boys use the front–left hemisphere of the brain to process and understand words, and, unlike boys, most girls can use both hemispheres of the brain to process and understand words. Girls have an advantage in a linear curriculum that relies on a verbal platform. Unlike boys, girls do not require physical movement to process information that is delivered via primarily auditory means, such as through lec-

The Rise of the Human Digital Brain:
How Multidirectional Thinking is Changing the Way We Learn, pages 27–36.

ture. Boys, on the other hand, tend to have brains that (in about 80% of males) are more spatial-mechanical and visual-graphic in nature. As noted in the previous chapter, this is due to the fact that the larger the amount of testosterone introduced in utero, the greater spatial-mechanical and visual-graphic skills an individual will develop. Less testosterone in utero will result in better verbal skills.

The greater the spatial-mechanical and visual-graphic skills, the greater the need to see the body as "an object moving through space" (Gurian, 2017a). For most boys, in order to keep the left hemisphere of the brain activated during lectures, the right hemisphere of the brain must also be activated. The way to accomplish this for most males is through movement. However, we continue to sit boys in a classroom, tell them to use their words, and discourage them from movement. We barely teach spatial intelligence in the classroom and defer to demonstrations of verbal intelligence for assessment of knowledge. This is unfair to boys who require movement to trigger the right hemisphere of the brain, thus stimulating the left hemisphere of the brain, which remains largely untriggered when seated at rest.

In addition to this, most females can learn to decode through both synthetic and analytic phonics. This means that they can learn to read using both sight words (analytic phonics) and phonetic sounds (synthetic phonics). Most boys learn to read best primarily through synthetic phonics. This means that boys may rely much more on the sense of hearing when learning to read than on the sense of sight (Johnston, Logan, & Watson, 2009). Because the key areas of white matter that are essential to the development of decoding skills develop between kindergarten and 3rd grade, a boy is more likely to lose ground if he develops frequent ear infections or experiences central auditory processing deficits during this time period. Research conducted in 2004 indicates that boys are two to three times more likely to have reading disorders than girls (Ritter et al., 2004). In the case of literacy, gender does indeed matter.

At the 2017 National Conference on Innovative Teaching Strategies, Dr. Michael Gurian stated that co-ed schools "are girls' schools that boys go to." The type of spatial-mechanical and visual-graphic learning that would enable boys to thrive is just not available in the current system of education in the United States. But how can we go about creating a system that is fair to both males and females?

BRAIN-BASED LEARNING

As noted in the first chapter of this book, thanks to modern advances in neuroscience, we know much more about how the brain processes information than we ever have before. We know that each brain is developed as a result of unique and individual experiences. Billions of events that occur throughout the course of a lifetime create physical changes in the brain and body. Our different experiences make each of us individualized in thought. Education is a field where our knowledge and understanding of the learning process could affect outcomes for future generations.

Initiatives are currently underway to bring the fields of neuroscience and education together to create a system that better fits the learning needs of the 21st century learner. The Economic and Social Research Council-funded seminar series "Collaborative Frameworks in Neuroscience and Education" was developed to help better understand the learning process (Greenfield, 2008). Brain-Based Learning Theory is another way for us to better understand the cognitive underpinnings of the learning process.

Brain-Based Learning Theory (BBL) suggests that "students should be provided a safe and threat-free environment whereby the meaningful presentation of content prepares the learners' brains to store, process and retrieve the information in a soothing way" (Ur-Rehman & Bokhari, 2011, p. 354). The BBL theory works under 12 basic principles:

1. The brain is a parallel processor.
2. The search for meaning is innate.
3. Learning engages the entire physiology.
4. The search for meaning occurs through "patterning."
5. Emotions are critical to patterning.
6. Every brain simultaneously perceives and creates parts and wholes.
7. Learning involves both focused attention and peripheral perception.
8. Learning always involves conscious and unconscious processes.
9. We have at least two types of memory systems: spatial and rote learning.
10. The brain understands and remembers best when facts and skills are embedded in natural spatial memory.
11. Learning is enhanced by challenge and inhibited by threat.
12. Every brain is unique (Ur-Rehman & Bohari, 2011, p. 355).

This framework suggests that learning will occur when individuals feel comfortable in an environment and when learning activates both conscious and unconscious processes and perceptions. It also suggests that learning occurs through patterning. Our brains automatically look for reoccurring patterns that can be connected and that will lead to synthesis. Additionally, because the brain functions as a parallel processor, it is designed to divide information among multiple processors to shorten the amount of time necessary for understanding to occur. When we compare this to computer processing, we know that before Windows was introduced, early computers (which used Microsoft DOS) only ran one program at a time, were very limited in ability, and took much more time to produce results (Hoffman, 2014). Eventually, computers had to become parallel processors to perform tasks with greater speed. By spreading the information into a variety of data streams, the time it took to process information was greatly reduced. This is similar to how learning occurs in the human brain, but it is not similar to current linear patterns that are prevalent in educational settings.

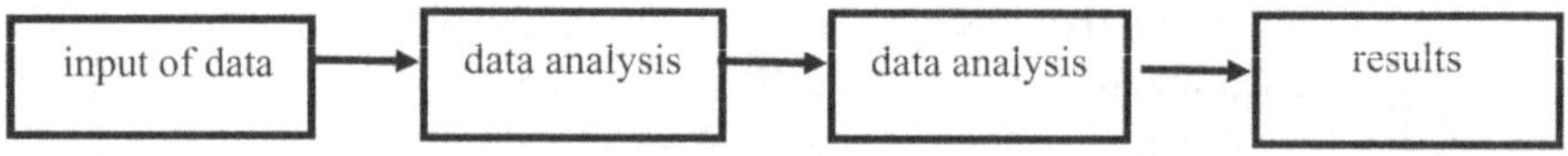

FIGURE 3.1. Linear thinking

The purpose of linear thinking is to allow information to be processed in a streamlined way to focus the mind on a single process. Figure 3.1 shows how linear thinking occurs.

This model looks much like the data processing centers of older computers that focused on one data stream at a time. However, if we think of the brain as capable of thinking in parallel, the model changes to one that can process multiple data streams simultaneously (see Figure 3.2 below).

Parallel processing, as it is defined in Brain-Based Learning Theory, relies on both conscious and unconscious processes. Unconscious processes include the use of the sensory memory to register information and to activate associated memory networks such as individual needs, beliefs, and desires. Conscious processes include learning that takes place when an individual deliberately pays attention to instructional materials and notices the similarities and differences between things (such as words and meanings). Information gathered through both conscious and unconscious processes is connected to prior experience and helps to build connections between the prior knowledge and the newly acquired knowledge. This has the potential to create new knowledge structures (Kuldas, Ismail, Hashim, & Bakar, 2013). These knowledge structures must be activated and built early, and they must be reinforced through proper instruction and repeated practice.

The image in Figure 3.2 represents a more integrative approach where information is being processed in a variety of ways and through a variety of senses all at once rather than being analyzed one piece at a time. Think about this in terms

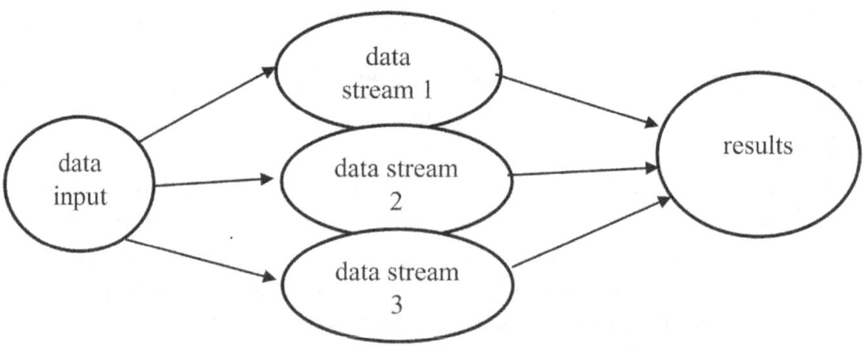

FIGURE 3.2 Parallel Processing (image adapted from "parallel processing" searchdatacenter.techtarget.com)

of a modern classroom. A lesson in an English class may focus on reading an assigned text. The student is asked to read the information and then answer questions regarding the reading. These questions are usually presented in line with the sequence of events in the story. This makes answering the questions rather simple as the questions and answers are presented in a sequential order, and it is a rather linear process. In this case, the main sensory input is visual.

According to Canadian professor and author Tom Wujek, the brain uses visual processing in three different ways to derive meaning. First, the eyes visually interrogate what is being observed. As the brain processes this visual image, it then splits it into figments of information and asks questions of each of these figments. A unified mental model is then created. According to Wujek, the act of engaging and creating interactive imagery enriches meaning by activating different parts of the brain during the process of visual interrogation, and this results in faster processing (Wujek, 2009).

We know that the reading process relies mainly on one sensory input, which is vision. What happens when a reader demonstrates decoding difficulties that slow down processing? When this is the case, presenting the information in the form of an auditory book that may be used in conjunction with a printed copy relies upon multiple senses to process the information rather than just one. This can speed up the process of comprehension, and it allows the brain to function as a parallel processor.

Comprehension will also be improved if students are given the opportunity to choose pieces of literature that are of interest to them. This may lead to more focused attention, which will also aid in more integrative processing because more connections are being made as the information is received.

VOCABULARY INSTRUCTION AND READING ACHIEVEMENT

According to a 2003 National Assessment of Educational Progress (NAEP) study, one-third to one-fourth of U.S. students do not have adequate basic reading skills (as cited in Rader, 2010). This lack of proficiency may be attributed to a lack of both oral language skills and vocabulary in children who have yet to start school. Susan B. Neuman, a professor of education at New York University, conducted a study in 2006 that focused on vocabulary attainment in pre-school children. Her results indicated that children need to build a vocabulary bank of at least 2,500 words per year from the age of three years and up. This creates a strong connection between cognitive development and language.

The development of these essential cognitive and language skills may require more time for boys to develop because girls tend to develop language more quickly than boys (James, 2015). Without proper vocabulary development, a child's Verbal Comprehension Index, which measures the ability to reason and solve problems verbally, may be negatively impacted. This could lead to lower success in academics even though a child may be of adequate intelligence.

Essential cognitive and language skills that have yet to develop in boys by the early grade school years may pose a challenge for educators attempting to develop effective literacy instructional strategies (Gurian & Stevens, 2007). Knowing how to read words, or simply decoding, which is considered a surface-level reading strategy, is of little value if a student is unable to create meaning. Because vocabulary and comprehension are considered deep-level reading strategies, the use of visual imagery could impact language attainment by bringing meaning to the text in a new way.

The process of visualization has been shown to significantly improve reading comprehension as it helps students to process, organize, and store new information as pictures and then to change those images back to words through the process of verbalization (Rader, 2010). This supports Brain-Based Learning Theory in that more of the physiology is engaged in the learning process when visualization skills are activated along with auditory and kinesthetic means of representation (Park, 2012).

According to Richard Mayer and Roxana Moreno (2003), learning processes refer mainly to "the interconnections between perception, memory, language, imagery, emotion, and motivation that allows a student to mentally review the connections between verbal and pictorial information patterns or between new and prior memories and integrate them with knowledge structures in the long-term memory" (as cited in Kuldas et al., 2013, p. 46). This definition offers some insight to good strategies for vocabulary instruction.

In school, educators rely quite a bit on the teaching of linear processes and forget that the complex brains in front of them are capable of processing things at a much faster rate if they can integrate information. Many teachers reinforce understanding of vocabulary by relying on rote memorization. Students often must "match the word to the definition." While this may allow the student to pass the test rather easily, it does not allow the student to fully embed meaning. To do this successfully, more senses must be activated. If students are given a visual picture of the word, a definition, a part of speech, and an example of the word used in a sentence, they now must engage in integrative thinking. Once this information is integrated and practiced, it is more likely to be stored in long-term memory. When it is necessary to retrieve this information, it is done more easily because a visual image may come to mind when the word is heard. This activates all the other information that has been stored along with it.

Figure 3.3 is an example of the use of an integrative process for the teaching of a single vocabulary word. The image in Figure 3.3 was selected because it is meant to clarify what is being communicated. The images that are selected for vocabulary instruction should augment memory by creating visual persistence so that the receiver successfully encodes the image. For this reason, it is best to let the instructor select the images initially, and then eventually, after explaining the purpose of the visuals, the instructor may allow students to select images to

Perceptive (adj) to grasp with the mind
Synonym: insightful

The **perceptive** child was able to understand the equation, even before his teacher explained how to find the answer.

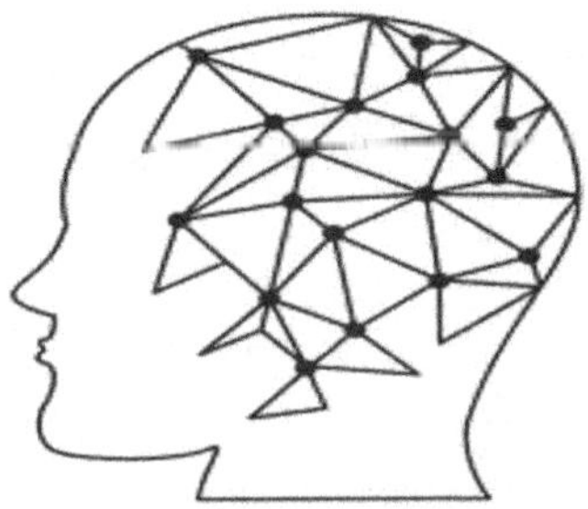

FIGURE 3.3. Vocabulary Slide

make the process more interactive and to create even greater awareness of word meaning.

To test this information, an integrative process must also be introduced. The student should be able to provide a definition in her own words (this does not need to be the definition word for word, and it may even simply be a synonym as the purpose is to demonstrate understanding rather than memorization) and then use that word effectively with good context clues and as the correct part of speech in a sentence. See the example in Figure 3.4. As opposed to a multiple-choice or matching test, this form of assessment activates higher-order thinking skills. The student will have to analyze the context of a sentence to determine which word will fit best, and then she will synthesize the information by creating a sentence with strong context clues. Most importantly, a mental picture of the word has been introduced and created for the student. I have used this method of vocabulary instruction and assessment for years, and I am always delighted when I hear a student say, several years after being in my class, that they can still see the picture from the vocabulary slides when they think of a particular word.

Other areas of brain-based learning that are not taken into to account in many classrooms today include the engagement of the entire physiology and the importance of spatial memory. As noted in earlier chapters, school was created to fit an industrial, linear society's needs. There was little reliance on the visual-spatial right hemisphere of the brain. Learning that takes place primarily through lecture does not activate the visual-spatial and mechanical reasoning areas of the brain found in the right hemisphere and relies heavily on the left hemisphere where language is centered. However, unless both areas of the brain are activated, creativity may be stymied. Boys in particular will better learn and understand information

<table>
<tr><th colspan="3">Part I—Parts of Speech/Definitions:</th></tr>
<tr><th>Word</th><th>Part of speech</th><th>Definition/Synonym</th></tr>
<tr><td>1. PERCEPTIVE</td><td></td><td></td></tr>
<tr><td></td><td></td><td></td></tr>
<tr><td></td><td></td><td></td></tr>
<tr><td></td><td></td><td></td></tr>
<tr><td colspan="3"></td></tr>
<tr><th colspan="3">PART II: Context clues</th></tr>
<tr><td colspan="3">Read the sentences below and fill in the blanks with the appropriate vocabulary words from the list above and write the words in the correct form:</td></tr>
<tr><td colspan="3">The young man was very ____________________, and he quickly figured out how to solve the Rubik's Cube after only seeing it done once.</td></tr>
<tr><td colspan="3"></td></tr>
<tr><td colspan="3"></td></tr>
<tr><td colspan="3"></td></tr>
<tr><th colspan="3">Part III</th></tr>
<tr><td colspan="3">Write meaningful sentences with good context clues for the following words:</td></tr>
<tr><td colspan="3">Perceptive (write as a complex sentence)</td></tr>
<tr><td colspan="3"></td></tr>
<tr><td colspan="3"></td></tr>
<tr><td colspan="3"></td></tr>
</table>

FIGURE 3.4. Vocabulary Quiz

if more of their physiology is incorporated into the learning activities. This is because, as noted earlier, 80% of males operate primarily from the right hemisphere of the brain, particularly when learning new concepts (Gurian, 2017b). If a student learns a subject such as biology primarily through lecture, he may memorize and regurgitate information that is stored in rote memory, but an active science lab where information is being put into practice will increase learning potential by activating the spatial memory as well. The theory that we learn best by doing is, therefore, a true statement.

BRAIN-BASED LEARNING AND SYSTEMS THEORY

According to Susan Greenfield, a British scientist and professor whose research includes the impact of technology on the brain, many parents and grandparents would like to see hard data identifying what impact screen time is having on our children. They also want to know if knowledge (as compared to knowledge gained by previous generations) is being lost. However, she believes that this focus is misguided. The focus on the impact of 21st century technology should be used to help us create a more effective 21st century educational system. She also believes that if both the public and private sectors work together to develop the best science and technology initiatives, we can coordinate on a nationwide scale.

In her book *ID: The Quest for Meaning in the 21st Century* (2008), Greenfield refers to the conceptual framework that was used in the 20th century model. This model was built upon a "means of evaluating current experience against ideas and generalizations previously elaborated and modified by reading books and endlessly cross-referencing them" (p. 284). While those of us educated in the 20th century and early 21st century may possess these skills, we cannot assume that children who have been exposed to technology since birth have the same innate abilities. The type of conceptual framework necessary to meet the needs of 21st century learners should harness screen technologies in addition to reinforcing more traditional methods.

Greenfield reminds us that because we now have access to current and relevant information at just the touch of a button (or a screen), we must focus on creating questions that are both meaningful and appropriate. Learning must develop into the type of integrative process that pulls in multiple senses. Abstract concepts, in particular, can be taught by a review of the many contexts to which they may be applied. For example, the concept of "freedom" could be researched and cross-referenced, and this would continue to activate the working memory in the process. This can help students to develop their own conceptual frameworks and also help them to formulate better questions about what "freedom" may mean in a variety of contexts.

Additionally, students must be directly and purposefully taught how to weigh information for authenticity. When a book or journal is published, it is usually peer-reviewed, and once it hits the shelves of stores, one can be relatively certain that the information contained in it is factual. This is not the case with information published on the internet. Some places where people choose to get their news today, such as Facebook and Twitter, are filled with false information that in many cases is designed to prey upon gullible readers who have not yet learned how to be discerning about the sources from which they choose to get their information. It is important that more learning standards be developed to address the skills of digital citizenship to help our youth understand that not everything that they read on a screen has been fully vetted for accuracy.

THE DYNAMISM OF THE HUMAN BRAIN

We now know that the brain has a great deal of neuroplasticity, which is defined as "the brain's ability to reorganize itself by forming new neural connections throughout life. Neuroplasticity allows the neurons (nerve cells) in the brain to compensate for injury and disease and to adjust their activities in response to new situations or to changes in their environment," (Neuroplasticity, 2018). One way that we see technology affecting this new generation is through its impact on their ability to relate to others. Children are now looking to sources that they are not yet equipped to fully vet for accuracy and authenticity. They are "meeting" each other via the internet, socializing on screens, and their brains are changing because of all these interactions.

In a 2017 article in *The Atlantic* entitled "Have Smartphones Destroyed a Generation," Jean Twenge, a researcher of generational differences, points out that we have seen dramatic shifts in behavior since 2012, the time when the proportion of Americans who owned smartphones surpassed fifty percent. Twenge refers to children born between 1995 and 2012 as the "iGen" because they grew up with smartphones, have had Instagram accounts before the start of high school, and cannot remember a time before the internet. This type of technology is ever-present in the lives of the iGen. In homes in the United States with children under the age of 9, ninety-eight percent have access to mobile devices, and a 2017 survey of more than 5,000 American teens determined that three out of four own an iPhone.

The advent of ubiquitous technology that is literally available from the time a person wakes up in the morning until she goes to bed at night has changed patterns of behavior as well as patterns of thought. The changes that have occurred have impacted the nature of social interactions as well as the state of mental health for our youth. Rates of teen depression and suicide have skyrocketed since 2011, while during the same period there has been a decline in teen homicides. Teenagers are now less likely to harm someone else but more likely to harm themselves. This is also impacting teens' abilities to relate to others. Eighty-five percent of high school senior Baby Boomers and Generation X'ers went out on dates; in 2015, that number was down to only fifty-six percent. While this decrease in face-to-face social interactions has had a positive impact on teen pregnancy rates, which reached an all-time low in 2016 and are down by sixty-seven percent from the modern peak in 1991, it is an indication of how isolated our youngest generation is becoming (Twenge, 2017).

According to Greenfield, we are potentially creating an identity crisis for our children because technology is redefining the way that they see themselves, what they want from life, and what makes them happy. She argues that the pervasive nature of the new technologies is exactly what makes them dangerous to young, malleable minds. The portable nature of technology has allowed us to remain constantly connected, but this also presents a new danger. Our very understanding of complex materials or scenarios may be endangered as we tend to simplify everything down to a 140-character (or more recently a 280-character) tweet.

Greenfield reminds us that there is no precedent in human history that might give us a clue as to what the outcome of this ubiquitous and pervasive technology might be, but one thing remains clear. The way that we think, the way that we socialize, and the very way that we feel is being changed by a small, hand-held screen that is exercising more and more control over our lives and is shaping the identity of our youth in ways that we cannot yet imagine.

CHAPTER 4

SYSTEMS THINKING AND 21ST CENTURY EDUCATION

Whom does our current educational system serve? According to information found on the XQ Super School website, American high schools currently have approximately 15 million students. Of these 15 million, 52% identify as White, 14.5% identify as Black, 25.9% identify as Latino, 5.5% identify as Asian/Pacific Islander, 1% identify as American Indian, and 2.5% identify as being of two or more races. Of these students, more than one in six (17%) is growing up in poverty and one in twenty needs help mastering English. Surprisingly, more than 95% of the students in the 9th grade, regardless of ethnicity or income level, are planning on attending college (Education Trust, 2017).

While the fact that students recognize the importance of education and the impact that it can have on their futures is impressive, not all of them are provided with equal access to the resources that can help them to get to the next level. The reality is that our schools do not educate all students in the same way. This is particularly true of students living in poverty and those of color. We spend about $2,000 less per student in school districts that have the highest populations of minorities. We also spend approximately $1,200 dollars less per student in school districts where the students with the highest levels of poverty reside. As if that weren't bad enough, there is evidence that students of color are actually receiving a lesser quality of education even when they are high achieving. For example,

The Rise of the Human Digital Brain:
How Multidirectional Thinking is Changing the Way We Learn, pages 37–44.

high achieving Black 8th graders are half as likely to be placed in Algebra 1 as equally high achieving White or Asian students. Additionally, students in schools serving mostly low-income students receive A's for work that would earn C's or B's in schools in more affluent school districts.

These inequities in quality of education and funding can have a devastating impact on student success. By the end of high school, 33% of Black students and 46% of Latino students are college ready in English compared to 73% of White students and 75% of Asian students. In math, only 13% of Black students and 30% of Latino students are considered college ready compared with 50% of White students and 75% of Asian students. These facts also impact college success. While 41% of White students will graduate with a bachelor's degree, only 23% of Black students and 19% of Latino students will achieve the same degree (Education Trust, 2017).

How can we affect a system that has remained largely unchanged for over one-hundred and fifty years in order to provide greater equity for all?

WHAT IS SYSTEMS THINKING?

Robert Pirsig in his work *Zen and the Art of Motorcycle Maintenance* cited in *Thinking in Systems: A Primer* (2008) by Donatella Meadows says: "If a factory is torn down but the rationality which produced it is left standing, then that rationality will simply produce another factory. If a revolution destroys a government, but the systematic patterns of thought that produced that government are left intact, then those patterns will repeat themselves...There's so much talk about system. And so little understanding."

This is a rather impactful statement as it helps us to realize that simply having the desire to change is not enough. For real change to occur, the patterns of thought of those who create the systems must also change.

To affect true change, we must first review the systems that exist with the purpose of promoting uniformity. According to Meadows, a system is "a set of things—people, cells, molecules, or whatever—interconnected in such a way that they perform their own pattern of behavior over time" (Meadows, 2008, p. 2). We are at a unique stage in human history where changes are occurring organically because of technology and its impact on the brain. As a result, we must consider engaging in systems thinking, which Meadows defines as "a way of thinking that will help us manage, adapt, and see the wide range of choices before us. It is a way of thinking that gives us the freedom to identify root causes of problems and see new opportunities" (Meadows, 2008, p. 2).

As noted throughout this book, technology encourages less linear and more multidirectional patterns of thought. The problem that we face today is that those who are teaching and those who are making decisions regarding the best ways to educate 21st century students were indoctrinated in systems designed to accommodate linear thinking. Baby Boomers and generation X'ers are not yet ready for the sweeping changes necessary to create successful reform because in order to fully embrace this change, they must be willing to admit that the system that led them to success is no longer viable.

MOORE'S LAW

In his novel *Thank You for Being Late* (2016), Thomas Friedman suggests that the world is not just being subjected to the type of normal change that previous generations have seen. The changes that are occurring today are happening more rapidly and across many disciplines at once. What makes the type of change occurring in the 21st century different from other major changes that have occurred throughout history is that the world is now being dramatically reshaped in many realms at once. Friedman asserts that there is a "mismatch between the pace of change and our ability to develop the learning systems, training systems, management systems, social safety nets, and government regulations that would enable citizens to get the most out of these accelerations and cushion their worst impacts" (p. 28).

Friedman cites Eric Teller, CEO of Google's X research and development lab, as a source who believes that the impact of Moore's Law and its acceleration are causing many of the ills found in today's current systems. Moore's Law was developed in 1965 when Gordon Moore, Intel co-founder, noticed that the number of transistors per square in integrated circuits doubled every year since their invention. He surmised that this type of "doubling" of technology could be predicted to occur every year, thus resulting in exponential growth. Teller explains that the scientific progress of the past, consisting of the introduction of things such as the printing press, the telegraph, and the typewriter, had an appropriate time lapse between their introduction and the time it took for them to become ubiquitous. Teller goes on to explain that a thousand years ago, scientific and technological progress rose very gradually, and it could take as long as one-hundred years for the world to look and feel different. Nothing really had a global impact all at once because there was so much time and space between people in different countries and on different continents.

By 1900, the process of technological and scientific change began to accelerate, and it was taking only 20 to 30 years for change to occur on a global scale. By 2016, this window of time for global change to occur was narrowed to five to seven years from introduction to global impact. This is due largely to innovations in technology that are easily spread through broadband connectivity, mobile devices, and even the introduction of "the cloud," where information can be stored and retrieved with great ease.

Teller also believes that there is a "competing curve," which is the rate at which humans are capable of adapting to changes in the environment. Over centuries, man has become better able to adapt more rapidly to global social and technological changes. The rate at which humans could adapt to change 1,000 years ago was two or three generations. By 1900, this was lowered to just one generation. In the current era, we may only require 10 to 15 years to adapt to change. Even though this is a large decrease in the learning curve, it is still not good enough for us to adjust to the rapid changes occurring in the 21st century. The acceleration in the speed of change that technology has brought about is outpacing the capacity of the average human to adjust to these changes. According to Teller, if it "takes us 10 to 15 years to understand a new technology and then build our new laws and regulations to safeguard society, how do we regulate when the technology has come and gone in five to seven years?" (Friedman, 2016, p. 33).

According to Friedman, one way to understand this is to recognize that we live in a primarily linear world because time, distance, and velocity are linear. We only experience exponential curves when something accelerates rapidly, like a car going from zero to sixty. Today's technology is on an exponential curve and not following the preferred linear patterns of past generations. As a result, Teller notes that the way that we educate our population also must change.

A new purpose of education must be to help society adapt to a rapidly changing world. In the 21st century, change constantly bombards us. The time lapse between the new information that we receive and the amount of time necessary to process and ingrain the changes is too short. By the time we have developed an understanding of a process, it may have already changed again. Teller goes on to suggest that we are now in a state of constant destabilization. Static stability no longer exists in today's day and age. This is resulting in a reinforcement of Piaget's concept of "cognitive disequilibrium."

COGNITIVE DISEQUILIBRIUM AND 21ST CENTURY EDUCATION

As noted in earlier chapters, cognitive disequilibrium occurs when we do not have in place an existing schema, or frame of reference, to refer to as we attempt to learn and understand new information. The goal of all learning is to achieve cognitive equilibrium. As a child begins to understand the world around him, he develops schemas (or stores of existing knowledge) by which to compare new input. For example, for a child to understand what a bird is, he first must realize that something with wings has the potential to fly. Things that fly are birds. Now the child can categorize things with wings as birds, and birds with the ability to fly. But what happens when a child sees a chicken and realizes that it cannot fly? He now must create a new schema within his existing schema. Now he knows that most things with wings can fly and that most things with wings are birds. He will continue to adjust this schema and form new schemas as more information is presented. However, if he has too much information provided all at once, this may challenge many different schemas simultaneously. This can lead to cognitive disequilibrium, which can lead to a sense of confusion and hopelessness.

Think about the technology that we use today. Can you list all the changes that have occurred since the iPhone was introduced just 10 years ago? Our iPhone is subject to so many daily updates that it is nearly impossible for the human mind to keep up with all these changes. This is particularly challenging for older individuals because to ingrain a new process, an existing schema may have to be removed and replaced by a new one. It is more difficult to let of go of old information to make room for new information because of our desire to hold on to patterns that are well-established and become a part of how we see ourselves in relation to the world.

FLOWS AND STOCKS

So how can we learn to think in patterns that will promote true change? First, we must begin to understand what drives our current system. Systems are made up of flows and stocks. For example, the knowledge that a teacher provides to his students would be considered a flow. If we consider the student an empty glass, we wait for the knowledge that the teacher imparts to this student to flow into the glass as a way for the student to increase his stock. The more knowledge provided, the greater the level of stock obtained by the student. If we think about this analogy and relate it to our current education system, we see that the goal is not always to increase the level of stock. Rather, the purpose seems to be to maintain dynamic equilibrium. What this means is that the goal of certain systems is actually to *prevent* the levels from changing, thus assuring that the status quo will be maintained. If the goal is to maintain the same level of water in each glass, systems will "buffer" in order to build in time to allow us to adjust to the changes.

Think of a bathtub being filled with water. If the tub is half-full and the plug is removed, but the same flow of water continues into the bathtub, the level may not change despite the continuous flow of water through it. If the flow remains constant, there is no need for change once a comfortable level has been reached. In the education system, these flows can be seen not only as knowledge, but also as funding. We have certain fixed budgets that are provided to schools, and as long as the amount going in remains equal to the amount going out, people find little reason to complain. Try to raise taxes to support the school system without raising wages, however, and people quickly recognize the change.

Additionally, the knowledge that students are expected to obtain is also strictly regulated. Common Core is one way of controlling this flow of knowledge to students. The flow will remain constant as long as the measures remain constant. If we continue to measure success by a list of pre-determined skills that has existed for over a century, then the stocks and flows will not change.

REINFORCING FEEDBACK LOOPS

Because we do recognize that change is inevitable, we have come to rely on the time lag between changes as a buffer. To facilitate this buffer, we rely on "reinforcing feedback loops." These types of feedback loops exist to "enhance whatever direction of change is imposed on it" (Meadows, 2008, p. 31). For example, taxes may have to go up, but if salaries do not go up, there is no reinforcing feedback loop to offset the change. If salaries also go up when a tax increase is imposed, eventually tax payers will adjust. However, they cannot be hit with a massive tax increase that is larger than income growth without causing a major disturbance in the system. In other words, we must create greater capacity for individuals to deal with the change before the implementation of the change can be successful. Government exists to regulate these changes and to make certain that the time lag between introduction of the change and its implementation is appropriate, but what happens when the time lag between the introduction of a large-scale change and its spread across the country or the globe is too short?

Reinforcing feedback loops occur so seamlessly and so often that it is easy to forget that "the exponential growth in stock resulting in a doubling of its size, referred to as "the 'doubling time,' equals approximately 70 divided by the growth rate (expressed as a percentage)" (Meadows, 2008, p. 33). Meadows provides the following example to illustrate this, "If you put $100 in the bank at 7% interest per year, you will double your money in 10 years (70 divided by 7 = 10). If you get only 5% interest, it will take 14 years to double" (Meadows, 2008, p. 33). In terms of the type of growth resulting from the use of technology that we are seeing in our stocks of knowledge, the time lag is shorter, and the amount of stock is increasing faster than any time in human history.

The time lag between introduction of new innovations and their spread is becoming shorter and shorter, and we have not educated our society to recognize this nor have we prepared them to adjust to these changes successfully. We have failed to realize that in modern society, there are now multiple flows of information, which Friedman refers to as "an acceleration of flows." The teacher in a classroom is no longer the "sage on the stage," or the main source of knowledge available to modern students. Students are now able to access information from multiple flows, such as the internet, applications, social media sites, and television, and thus the stock can no longer maintain dynamic equilibrium. If we think of the student's mind as a hard drive, as opposed to an empty glass, we may develop a better understanding of the needs of the 21st century students.

STABILIZING FEEDBACK LOOPS

A hard drive, unlike an empty glass, contains multiple "platters" or compartments where data is written using a magnetic head. This information is spread across the entire hard drive, and information can be synthesized into new information when it is retrieved. The most important difference between the glass analogy and the hard drive analogy is that the goal is no longer dynamic equilibrium. We do not have a set amount of knowledge that can be obtained before the glass overflows and a mess is created. There is much more information that can be added to the "stock" of a hard drive, and the capacity to hold larger amounts of information is growing. If we keep in mind the multiple flows available to our students in 21st century classrooms, the new goal of education should be defined by the higher-order thinking skills of analysis, synthesis, and evaluation as identified in Bloom's Taxonomy rather than reliance on lower-order thinking skills of knowledge, comprehension, and application. In other words, our goal should be to help students to effectively analyze all the inputs that they receive and then develop new schemas to understand this information and create new ideas as a result of this information.

We must also have as one of our goals as 21st century educators to create a better understanding of stabilizing feedback loops and how they should be viewed in light of modern advances in technology. The purpose of a stabilizing feedback loop in a system is to stabilize the stock level. While the level of stock may not always remain consistent, it is held at an acceptable level by stabilizing feedback loops. For example, if you feel your energy waning, you may stop to eat a snack to maintain dynamic equilibrium. If you don't eat, your stock will continue to lower, and you may feel weak until you are able to replenish your stock. Because the stock of knowledge is now increasing at such an exponential rate, we risk gorging ourselves on this information. There is not enough time for the brain to process all this information effectively, and stabilization becomes nearly impossible. Using the analogy of food as the input, we know that if we eat too much, our bodies begin to feel ill and have difficulty processing the large intake effectively. But if we choose to be selective in what we eat, making certain that what we digest in larger quantities is healthy for our bodies and is taken in moderation rather than saturation, we will get stronger and healthier.

The same is true of the information that we digest. We need to be selective in what we take in and how we process it. We must slow down the mind to help it compartmentalize the information, process it, and then attach it to prior knowledge. This will result in the kind of synthesis and analysis that can promote true growth. It is also different from the type of dynamic equilibrium currently reinforced by the prevailing models in our modern education system. While the current model encourages stabilization through the application of group averages (everyone gets the same amount of the same type of information at the same time based on what is deemed best for the average individual), dynamic equilibrium does not have to be the same for each individual. When we apply the "glass have full" theory to dynamic equilibrium, it is important to remember that what goes into my glass to attain equilibrium does not have to be the exact same thing that goes into the glass of another.

According to Teller, achieving a new state of equilibrium will take substantial relearning. This is already happening in some universities across the United States as they experiment with a faster turnover of curriculum to better adjust to the pace of change. Gone are the days when we can reuse the same lesson plans and the same tests again and again. Educators must be just as dynamic and capable of change as those sitting in the seats in front of them.

DATA-DRIVEN LEARNING

In one chapter of the book *Change We Must: Deciding the Future of Higher Education* (Goldstein & Otte, 2016), Roy Schroeder and Vickie Cook discuss data-driven learning. They suggest that meaningful quantitative data should be gathered on each student to enable descriptive analytics to be used to help instructors better understand student characteristics and learning behaviors. This data should then be used to create prescriptive analytics. These prescriptive analytics would serve a purpose similar to a medical prescription for medication used to regulate the body. Prescriptive analytics would, in this capacity, be used to help recommend a variety of learning interventions that have demonstrated success with students of similar characteristics and circumstances. Universities can also use prescriptive analytics to create individualized learning plans for students that will accelerate their growth in areas of academic focus. These newer modes of education can lead to higher-order learning activities as students create products based on facts and formulas that are often learned online. Students will no longer rely solely on textbooks, and they are able to utilize professional resources to support their findings.

This is simply one example of how technology may be used to change our system for the better. Matthew Goldstein and George Otte, editors of *Change We Must: Deciding the Future of Higher Education* (2016), discuss not what *will* happen in higher education in the future but what *should and must* happen. While they readily admit that there is no quick fix, they realize that the time for change is now. The book contains a section focused on how the larger world impacts what should be taught and learned. Otte and Goldstein assert that "Change must be made deliberatively, effectively, decisively. Change in short, must be managed." So how do we manage unprecedented change in a system that was designed to promote uniformity? We must create a new understanding of equilibrium. We must no longer be content with the concept that equilibrium is the same for everyone. Standing still is not an option. We must learn to survive in a world that is in perpetual motion. Like riding a bicycle, we must find a balance that will allow us to stay upright while anticipating bumps and road blocks. If effectively reinforced, this type of learning can change the trajectory of human history.

CHAPTER 5

THE MULTIDIRECTIONAL MIND

How It Is Emerging and What It Means

Before attempting to contemplate how to flip an entire system that has existed in the same form for hundreds of years, it is important to gain a true understanding of the changes that are occurring. What does "multidirectional thinking" really refer to, and how can we better understand its implications?

What we know about how the brain develops centers on how patterns of attention shape thought. The adult brain has been estimated to contain more than one-hundred-billion neurons, and throughout most of the 20th century, it was believed that the number of neurons in each human brain would increase with time and age. That assumption is incorrect, however. In reality, the brain has about 40% less neurons when we are adults than it did when we were infants. These neurons in the brain can connect to up to 10,000 other neurons via synaptic connections, which are small gaps separating neurons and that facilitate communication between the neurons. When certain neurons are not used, the brain does away with the unused links to free up more space for information that is more relevant (Davidson, 2011).

The more we repeat certain patterns of behavior, the more likely we are to develop automaticity. Driving and reading are two examples of complex activities that rely on the development of automaticity, or the ability to perform certain ac-

The Rise of the Human Digital Brain:
How Multidirectional Thinking is Changing the Way We Learn, pages 45–52.

tions automatically without having to stop and reflect on each part of the process. This happens in an effort to create efficiency. These patterns or habits are developed through learned processes. What we determine is important to our survival is what we will focus upon.

Because we know that the technology of today has ushered in a transformational period in human history, we must also acknowledge that this transformation is affecting what we pay attention to and why we pay attention to it. Technology is a tool, and as such, we must recognize its specific purpose in order to capitalize on it and use it efficiently. But what happens if its purpose is multifaceted? For example, a hammer is a tool that is used to maximize pressure so that nails may be driven into walls. The opposite side of the head of the hammer is designed to create leverage if a nail needs to be removed from a wall. Does the fact that the hammer has more than one use make it less effective as a tool to drive nails into walls? In this case, it probably has very little impact on our understanding of the purpose of the tool. But what happens when a tool has many different possible purposes, and those purposes keep changing on a daily basis? The technology that we use today has much more than one specific purpose and use. That purpose and use is constantly changing (thanks to technology updates and additions of new applications), and this is impacting the way that the brain perceives this tool. Does this fact impact and change the way that we learn?

F. Scott Fitzgerald, author of the iconic novel *The Great Gatsby*, saw "the ability to hold two opposing ideas in the mind at the same time and still retaining the ability to function" as the sign of a truly intelligent individual (Martin, 2007). With the changes in the amount of flows available, from classroom teachers to the internet, YouTube videos, Khan Academy, iPad and iPhone applications, and the multitude of other resources that may be accessed at the mere touch of a finger, the stocks created from these flows have changed. There is a broader array of information available, so not everyone develops the same stock of accepted information. This new system of learning has led to the decline of the linear model and the emergence of multidirectional thinking. Multidirectional thinking is characterized by the fact that it allows individuals to hold several opposing ideas in the mind at the same time and to make new and exciting connections that encourage creativity and ingenuity.

A good modern example of multidirectional thinking is the NBC television show *This Is Us*. This show provides the viewer with an opportunity to delve into the dynamics of a typical American family and to witness all their joy as well as their dysfunction. What makes this show different is its presentation. We are not told the story in a linear fashion. It does not start at the beginning and progress to a logical end. It starts in medias res, which is Latin for "in the middle of things." It starts with the birth of three babies, triplets. One of the triplets dies, and the distraught parents adopt a third baby who was abandoned on the same day that their children were born. From here, it jumps to the adult children's lives. As the story continues, the audience can be taken to any point in time in any of the character's lives (to include the parents or even minor characters who briefly impact their lives). This storyline works, and the series has high ratings and has garnered multiple Emmy nominations exactly because of its multidirectional nature. When we can't logically connect the dots, we become creative in our assumptions about what may have occurred. We are then excited to see if the actual outcomes match what we envisioned. But why is this type of thinking appealing to people, particularly in this day and age?

MULTIDIRECTIONAL THINKING AND INTEGRATIVE PROCESSES

According to Roger Martin's 2007 *Harvard Business Review* Article entitled "How Successful Leaders Think," we spend too much time focusing on what a leader does and not enough time focusing on how he thinks. Martin tries to explain how a leader's cognitive processes produce his actions. To explain this, he discusses the concept of synthesis. Martin believes that the best leaders "have the predisposition and the capacity to hold in their heads two opposing ideas at once." What makes these leaders different is what they determine to do with that information. They take the time to see all the moving parts, and instead of picking one idea over another, they take parts that they like from one model and parts from another until they have synthesized the information and created a new option. Martin refers to this type of thinking as "integrative thinking," and he believes that it tremendously improves the odds of success.

While I do tend to agree with Martin, I believe that the advances in technology since 2007 have created opportunities to hold more than two opposing ideas at once. Because of technology, it is now possible to hold several opposing ideas in the mind at once and to explore the connections between those ideas more quickly with the help of technology. This is what would be termed as multidirectional thinking. We not only divert from the linear process, but we also seek information by looking at similarities and differences between ideas, and we are willing to follow those connections wherever they may take us. What results is not just "integrative thinking," as Martin suggests. What occurs are integrative processes resulting from multidirectional thinking. We create processes that integrate a variety of methods based on what we learned from our multidirectional thought processes.

This can be used to understand a television show such as *This Is Us* because technology has allowed us to move in any direction that we choose, and this is exactly what the show does. Think of an iPad screen. You are provided with a menu of opportunities as soon as you access the screen, and you are not obligated to move in a linear direction. You can choose to start at the top of the screen, the middle, or the bottom (depending on what you need to know or want to do). This is affecting the brain by reinforcing these multidirectional processes. What eventually connects these choices are the reasons that we are looking for information. Most searches revolve around certain themes.

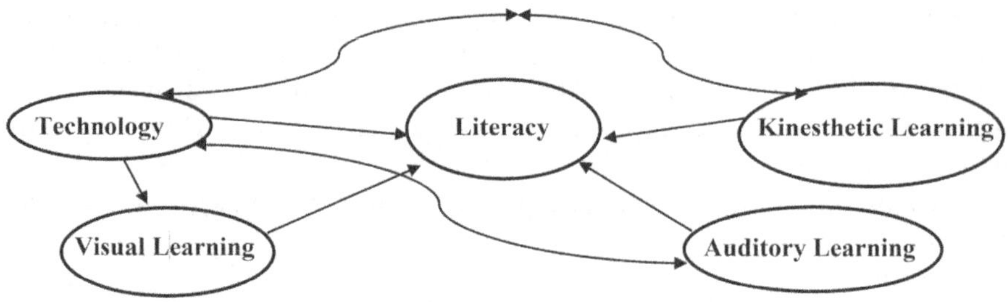

FIGURE 5.1. Synthesizing and Integrating

In the show *This Is Us,* there is a connection between themes in the story, but in terms of how it moves through time and space, that is left totally up to the storyteller. The themes are what connects all the stories: the love that we share knows no boundaries; family *can* be chosen; kindness matters; everyone struggles with self-doubt. All of these themes are tied to the story of one family that has multiple connections to friends, extended family, a fireman who finds a baby abandoned at the firehouse, and a doctor who delivers triplets and has to tell the parents that one did not survive. All these stories are woven together, or integrated, based on these themes, and they are understood and capture the attention of the audience. So how can we make school more like this?

When I began thinking about ways to increase comprehension skills for my students, I started with one concept, literacy. I then thought about all of the things associated with literacy, such as phonics, vocabulary, and fluency. I next looked at the sensory opportunities used to gain those skills: sight, sound, kinesthetic opportunities. All of these were available via the iPad. Now I had two central themes: literacy and technology (or more specifically, the iPad). All these concepts flowed together. Then came applications (or apps) that could be used to integrate visual, auditory, and kinesthetic opportunities. Features available via the iPad, such as change of screen background, font size, as well as auditory opportunities, were integrated into the process. The measure used to determine growth was the Nelson-Denny Reading Test, and it was already being consistently used, but the fact that the measure was linear in design and was not consistent with the mode of learning reinforced by the iPad led me to believe that the results might be skewed. Once I received the results, which I will provide with greater detail in chapter 10, they did indicate a growth in comprehension and vocabulary scores between pre- and post-tests, but compared to pre-iPad comprehension and vocabulary scores, there was a decline in growth of both skills, so I began to look for causes. I determined that the answer would not be a complete return to linear processes, nor would it be a complete shift to multidirectional processes. The answer would be a synthesis of the two processes.

HOW MULTIDIRECTIONAL THINKING LOOKS IN A 21ST CENTURY CLASSROOM

One thing that we all know about the process of learning is that we will pay attention to things that interest us. If we pay attention to something, we are more likely to create more elaborate and lasting connections between neurons. One of the best ways to help a 21st century learner is to find a way to connect his interests to his learning.

Because I work at a high school whose population is all male, I realized that reading would probably not be something that most of the students would be passionate about. I had to actively look for ways to develop that passion in them. One way that I chose to do this was by attending American Library Association conferences that focused on new literature for young adults. I took note of the newest books with themes that would appeal to male audiences. I then went back to my school with a list of books that we needed to acquire for our school's library. I was fortunate in that my school valued this process and provided the necessary funds to build our library. Additionally, our wonderful librarian worked with me to create a library filled with boy friendly literature. We also made sure to include specific titles for boys classified as "low-achieving readers" due to their demonstrated lack of proficiency in vocabulary and comprehension skills. This is a population that, for a variety of reasons, did not meet benchmarks in reading in grade school and had, in most cases, developed a distaste for reading in general. The hope was that, by providing literature of choice in subjects of interest to them, we would bridge that gap and help them develop a love (or at the very least a like) for reading.

The titles and cover photos of the books that were acquired by the school were then organized into a PowerPoint where links to a synopsis of each book could be found. This PowerPoint was made accessible to all students through a shared media platform. Students were then encouraged to review the PowerPoint before going to the library. Students were asked to find no less than three books of interest to consider checking out from the library. The students would then go to the library armed with the titles of those three top choices, and after looking through and reviewing each of the books, they would each check one of those choices out to read over a three-week period. A reading project that would promote visual, auditory, and kinesthetic opportunities for demonstration of understanding of the book would then be assigned.

This process proved to be successful because students now had choice and ownership in their reading. This was just one step in creating more avid readers, however. I have always believed that if you could hook a student on just one good book, you were taking the first step in creating a more successful reader. I found this to be true, and the results that were obtained using this method were truly beyond expectations. However, that process had to be reinforced in other ways as well.

HOW TO ENGAGE A NON-READER

One example of progress that can be made by using multisensory/multimodal processes is the progress a student who came to me his freshman year with a reading score on his entrance exam below the 5th percentile was able to demonstrate. This young man told me quite explicitly that he did not enjoy reading and that he was not good at it. I asked him what he felt his chief strengths were. He told me that he was a good artist. As we began our first group novel, I knew that I could capitalize on this student's passion for art. This particular student's group was reading a novel entitled *The Killer's Cousin* by Nancy Werlin. I made an assignment asking that the group create a visual depiction of the events of the story. They were to create a trifold with a plot pyramid representing rising action, climax, and falling action in the story as well as information about characters, setting, internal and external conflict and specific quotes to support a common theme in the story. I tasked this particular student with coming up with a vision for how these boards should look. He was to concentrate specifically on the descriptions and details of important events in the story and to figure out ways to represent them in a way that would catch the attention of an audience that would hear a presentation about this story. He took the challenge to heart, and what resulted was beyond my expectations.

This budding young artist painted the boards with a blue background surrounded by white, fluffy clouds made of cotton. He then had the other boys in his group type the information for the rising action, climax, and falling action on their iPads and print this information out for him. Next, he created a 3D model of the house that was the main setting in the book. He created the house from cardboard, and he carefully cut out open windows. The pitch of the roof served as the outline for the plot pyramid, and once the house was painted and placed in front of the boards, it looked impressive. He quickly reminded me that the house burns down towards the end of the story. He then turned on a small fan inside of the house, and flames (made of lightweight, carefully cut red fabric) began to blow out from the open windows! He had paid meticulous attention to the details of the setting, and he recreated it very accurately. This allowed me to see that he was creating a "mental movie" as he read the story. When the presentation was over, he told me, "Honestly, that's the first book I have ever read completely."

What makes this story even more amazing is that this young man went on to score a 21 in reading on the ACT (without any accommodations) his junior year. He became active in the process of reading. He was reading with a purpose, and he engaged in visual learning, auditory learning, and kinesthetic learning. This new "habit" was the result of new connections forming between neurons as a result of his application of his love of art to the process of reading. This was a process that he repeated again and again with each new book that he read.

Another example of this type of multidirectional learning is what occurred when a student in one of my freshman English classes was introduced to the short story "To Build a Fire" by Jack London. I had the students watch the movie in order to make certain that a mental picture was created. I then tasked them with writing a one-page journal entry for "the man" in the story detailing his final day. My hope was that my students would be able to demonstrate that they could recall specific events from the story and place them in the correct linear progression, a lower-order thinking skill.

The day that this assignment was due, this particular student proclaimed, "I think I did the assignment wrong." I prepared myself for an excuse, but instead, he said, "I wrote three pages instead of one." When I asked him why, he indicated that he felt that he really needed to experience for himself what the man in the story went through before he could write about it. He then went on to explain that he had a survival themed video game at home that allowed him to put in certain settings and conditions. He tried to replicate the conditions and setting of the story, and then he walked through it as a character in the game. He then wrote about his experiences as he traveled through the game. This student had a diagnosed Reading Disorder as well as a Disorder of Written Expression, but you would never know it if you read what he wrote. It was imaginative, demonstrated a clear plot, internal and external conflict, and the imagery was outstanding! He had connected his reading to something that he enjoyed, and this allowed him to synthesize the information from the story to create his own skillfully written journal. He had taken an assignment aimed at lower-order thinking skills of knowledge and comprehension and turned it into a lesson focused on the higher order thinking skills of analysis and synthesis. I had to share this with the class, and I told him that I was so proud of his demonstration of 21st century thinking skills by integrating technology with his learning process.

What both examples demonstrate is the application of focused attention. To build new neural pathways during adolescence, a time when the brain is busy pruning away connections that it deems unnecessary, it is crucial to apply focused attention to the skill. This means finding a way to help the student devote their complete attention to the task, like many boys will do willingly when it comes to playing a video game. To garner this focused attention, the learning must be connected to something important to the individual.

If you have ever had a sick pet who required medication, you know how important it is to hide something bitter inside of something sweet. Dogs, for instance, pay attention to food. It is what they love. To get them to do what they may hate over and over again (until all of the medication is gone and the dog is better), what do we usually do? We hide the medication in a tasty bit of food that the dog will find irresistible. Although this seems like a rather unrelated analogy, I think that it truly applies here. Think of how much a low-achieving adolescent reader must hate reading. How can you get him to apply focused attention to doing something over and over again in order to establish a new pattern? You need to hide it in something he loves. For one student it was art and for the other it was video games.

WHAT THIS MEANS FOR OUR FUTURE

In the futuristic novel *Fahrenheit 451*, written by Ray Bradbury in 1951 and published as a full novel in 1953, books have become illegal. In this dystopian society, firemen exist to find and burn books rather than to put fires out. The reason that books are burned in this story is to destroy any evidence of the original sources. History can be rewritten if there is no record of original sources, and in this story, full advantage is taken of a screen-driven society where characters in television shows are referred to as "family." One fireman, Montag, sees the error in this and attempts to save his own humanity from the perils of technology. While this novel seemed far-fetched in 1951, today it is becoming closer to reality than ever previously thought possible. With the modern advent of the term "fake news," we are seeing the first signs of attempts to rewrite the narrative through the active use of technology.

As we continue to look forward to technology-influenced future, we must allow our students to freely express their creativity, but we must also teach linear processes purposefully and help our students to understand the importance of using accurate and original sources to avoid the consequences suffered by the character of Montag in Bradbury's *Fahrenheit 451.* If educators can practice doing both things, the potential for intellectual growth can be as exponential as the growth of technology predicted by Moore's Law. If we fail to do both, we risk losing the potential and creativity contained within our youth.

CHAPTER 6

LEARNING DISABILITY OR LEARNING DIFFERENCE?

Changes in our behavior resulting from our screen-based lives are being observed in a variety of ways. Susan Greenfield, author of *ID: The Quest for Meaning in the 21st Century* (2008), believes that shorter attention spans and reduced personal communication skills are the direct result of a technology driven world. She also notes that abstract thinking, a higher-order thinking skill, is reduced as a direct result of so much screen time. Greenfield goes on to explain that the brain is malleable and is shaped by experiences. This "shaping" occurs at a microcellular level, and the complex network of nerve cells that make up parts of the brain are changing in response to experiences and stimuli. While most of the brain's plasticity is reserved for childhood, the brain does have the ability to change up to early adulthood and beyond. Just as pharmaceutical drugs can impact the way a person feels, electronic devices can also impact our thoughts and emotions.

Greenfield believes that the modern world could well be altering our human identity. She indicates that environmentally influenced changes have occurred throughout history, but today's challenges are much greater than those faced by previous generations. Thanks to social media, our very sense of self is impacted by not just those around us, such as our family, our friends, and our community, but also by people we may have never actually met. Because social media allows us to connect with anyone, anywhere, anytime, our sense of self is now connected

The Rise of the Human Digital Brain:
How Multidirectional Thinking is Changing the Way We Learn, pages 53–60.

to the comments being made by people who do not even know us or understand our values.

This constant search for affirmation (in the form of likes or followers) is a result of the dopamine release that occurs when we experience something pleasurable. This can become like a hamster on a wheel, and the mind is constantly running and ruminating on things that, in the grand scheme of things, are of little importance. This mirrors commonly known addictions such as alcohol or drug abuse in that the purpose of drinking alcohol or taking drugs is often to stimulate the pleasure centers of the brain. The same effect on the brain occurs with addiction to technology. The brain is not built to maintain a constant pleasure high and coming back to reality can lead to a crash that can be both mentally and physically exhausting. To maintain this artificial "high," an individual who is addicted to technology must try to stay constantly connected. As Greenfield asserts, the very sense of identity of the individual is being challenged on a daily basis, and this sense of self is, in many cases, tied to a small hand-held device that now has the power to shape the thoughts of the individual.

The need to remain constantly connected has been associated with poor social skills, lower grades, and a decline in health. There is also now circumstantial evidence to support the belief that the continuous use of technology has led to an increase in the diagnoses of Attention Deficit Hyperactivity Disorder (ADHD) (Greenfield, 2008).

According to a 2016 article in *Education Week* entitled "Number of U.S. Students in Special Education Ticks Upward," the number of students covered under the 2004 Individuals with Disabilities Education Act (IDEA) was at a low of 5.67 million if the fall of 2011. That number rose to 5.83 million by the fall of 2014, which is the most recent year with available statistics. What is most startling about the statistics compiled is the fact that students classified as having autism rose 165% between the 2005–2006 and 2014–2015 school years. Students classified as having "other health impairments," such as ADHD, increased by over 51% during the same 10-year time span. While there are numerous factors that may contribute to this increase, one thing remains certain. The individual needs of students are still not being adequately met in classrooms across the United States. In an attempt to meet those needs more specifically, more students are being tested for and diagnosed with learning disabilities.

THE AMERICANS WITH DISABILITIES ACT

The American's with Disabilities Act (ADA) defines a person with a disability as "a person who has a physical or mental impairment that substantially limits one or more major life activity. This includes people who have a record of such impairment, even if they do not currently have a disability," (American's With Disabilities Act, § 12102, 1990). The mandates of the American's with Disabilities Act as they pertain to meeting the needs of individuals with physical handicaps are commonly known and recognizable. We are used to seeing ramps for wheelchairs, elevators for access to various levels of buildings, wheelchair accessible bathrooms, and handicapped parking spots, but how do accommodations look for students with learning disabilities?

Our predilection towards linear thinking again informs the way that we address these types of disabilities. We often look for a "one size fits all" approach. While an individual in a wheelchair will always benefit from the use of a ramp to access buildings, an individual with ADHD is not always going to respond effectively to the exact same accommodations as another individual with the same disorder. However, in classrooms across the country, this type of standardization is exactly what is taking place. Accommodations for ADHD are typically extended time and preferential seating. While these accommodations may be a start, they do not meet the specific needs of all students with learning disabilities.

The irony of this really hit me when I was proctoring the PSAT in October of 2017. I had a group of students with the accommodation of extended time in one room. They started their test at 8:00 a.m. and finished their test at approximately 1:15 p.m. These students had short breaks between tests, but they did not have lunch provided because the test was scheduled to end at around noon for those taking the test without extended time. As we got closer to noon, I noticed that these students, many of whose diagnosed disability is ADHD, which often means that they may have difficulty paying attention for extended periods of time, were indeed becoming less and less engaged in the test. They were hungry and tired. Rather than providing them with an advantage that could help them put forth their best effort, it appeared that the accommodations that College Board was providing them with to mitigate their learning disabilities were in reality serving to exacerbate the problems.

MITIGATING THE EFFECTS OF LEARNING DISABILITIES

Barbara Arrowsmith Young, co-founder of the Arrowsmith School in Toronto and author of the 2012 book *The Woman Who Changed Her Brain*, was born in the 1950s. She is what we today would consider "twice exceptional," which is a term that is often used to describe children who are gifted but also have some form of disability. Barbara's auditory and visual memory both tested in the ninety-ninth percentile. She had remarkably well-developed frontal lobes, and this led to her being a very driven individual. She also had a brain that was "asymmetrical," which means that her exceptional abilities also coexist with areas of extreme weakness. The learning disabilities that Barbara struggled with included difficulty pronouncing words, lack of spatial reasoning skills, and kinesthetic problems. As a result, Barbara had difficulty telling her right hand from her left, she reversed letters, she wrote from right to left, and she could memorize math procedures but could not understand math concepts. She also had difficulty forming mental maps and frequently lost things. She was very clumsy, and her span of vision was so narrow that she had trouble understanding grammar, cause and effect, and logic (Doidge, 2007).

Barbara learned how to use her memory to mitigate her deficits. She could remember information if she practiced it over and over again, but remediation attempts, for the most part, did not aid her. Barbara lived in a time when her disabilities were misunderstood, and despite her giftedness, she was placed in "opportunity classes," which were reserved for children with severe disabilities, and not much was expected academically of these individuals. Barbara became frustrated with this, and she was determined to be successful. Her own perseverance and hard work led to her retraining her brain to by-pass her deficits. Despite having to re-read material up to twenty times in order to understand it, Barbara eventually graduated with a master's degree in psychology from the University of Toronto. While a student there, her professors had difficulty believing that she suffered from learning disabilities. Barbara proved that by using focused attention to exercise her most weakened functions, she could overcome her disabilities. She has developed a school designed to identify which brain functions are weakest and then to assign exercise programs aimed at mitigating (or even eliminating) the negative effects of these disabilities (Doidge, 2007).

One important piece of information that is crucial to understanding how Barbara was able to do this is the difference between critical-period plasticity and adult plasticity. A brain that is somewhat organized in childhood (as Barbara's was due to her early self-directed brain training) has the potential to learn how to sort out what is important to pay attention to and what is not (Doidge, 2007). When we reach adolescence, the brain is busy pruning away neural connections that are no longer necessary. During this time period, Barbara was practicing the very skills where her deficits existed, thus strengthening new neural pathways. Once she became an adult, she applied the same focus to her learning. Eventually, new areas of her brain trained themselves to take over functions that were impaired in other areas of the brain.

AUTISM

Autism has been classified as one of the most severe developmental disorders of childhood. It is also referred to as "Pervasive Developmental Disorder," because so many different areas of development are impaired, to include intelligence, perception, social skills, language, and emotion. Most children identified as autistic have difficulty connecting socially with others, and they may be hypersensitive to touch and sound. Too much stimulation in any form can be upsetting for an autistic child. Many children identified as autistic also have language impairments. Dr. Merzenich began to refer to autism as an "infantile catastrophe" because he believed that it occurred because of something that happens during infancy, a critical period of brain plasticity (Doidge, 2007). We do know that autism is, in most cases, an inherited condition, but this does not explain why incidences of autism have been steadily growing over the last few decades.

Merzenich believes that there may be environmental factors that affect the neural circuits in autistic children, and this causes critical-plasticity periods to shut down too early, before brain maps are fully formed and differentiated. He reviewed the work by Rita Levi-Montalcini, who won the Nobel Prize along with Stanley Cohen in 1986 for their work in isolating the protein responsible for the growth of nerves. One of the factors that was identified because of their work was brain-derived neurotrophic factor, called BDNF. Merzenich was interested in this particular nerve-growth factor because BDNF is released when neuron's fire and then wire together. When BDNF is released, it turns on the nucleus basalis, which helps us to pay attention and remember things. When BDNF is done strengthening important connections in the brain, it also helps to brain to close a critical-plasticity period. However, if something over excites the neurons in children who are predisposed to autism, BDNF may be released prematurely and in massive amounts. As a result, critical-brain plasticity periods are closed too early, and many of the forming brain maps remain undifferentiated. This leads to brains that are hypersensitive (Doidge, 2007).

This is probably easier to understand when you think of all the things that an infant has to learn in the first two years of life. During these first two years, the world is new, and the brain is designed to pay attention to everything. It does not yet know how to discriminate between what is important and what is not. As the brain grows and creates important neural connections, it begins to become more focused. Once the appropriate connections are made and focus is established, brain maps are formed and differentiated. When this critical-plasticity period is interrupted and shuts down before the maps have been differentiated, the brain remains at a heightened sense of awareness and has difficulty differentiating between what is important to pay attention to and what is not. For example, a simple sound may be amplified, and an individual with autism may not be able to isolate the sound from the other things that are occurring. Additionally, an individual with autism may have difficulty reading non-verbal cues (such as facial expressions) because he cannot differentiate them from the other cues that are being received. In short, the brain has difficulty knowing exactly what to pay attention to, so it tends to pay attention to everything.

LEARNING DISABILITY OR LEARNING DIFFERENCE?

The term "disability" often creates a mental image of a person who is unable to do something that most are capable of doing without the aid of assistance. However, this term can be very misleading. While it must be used on official or legal documentation for an individual to receive certain types of assistance, it suggests something negative due to its prefix "dis," which implies that a disability is the direct opposite of an ability. For example, if I have the ability to write information down using a pen and pencil, and you do not, you may have a disability known as dysgraphia. However, a person with dysgraphia Is not *incapable* of writing, and they do not have the *inability* to write, but that seems to be exactly what we think of when we hear the term "disability." I know many individuals with dysgraphia, and they all have the ability to write—it may just take them longer to get the information down on paper, or it may be a little more difficult to decipher what they have written, but they do have the ability to do it. I would say that what they need is *differentiation* to perform this task more efficiently. Things just need to be presented a little bit differently for them, but with the proper accommodations, they can take notes and put information in proper format just as well as anyone else. If differentiation is what is required, then perhaps this should be termed a "learning difference" rather than a "learning disability."

We all have learning differences, and if our needs are accommodated, our outcomes will improve. In traditional 21st classrooms, however, little attention is given to this fact. A student who requires that something be done differently to assist with her learning requires a 504, an IEP, or an Accommodation Plan. To get an accommodation, it is often required that expensive psychological/educational testing be done to establish the fact that a "disability" does exist. In the United States, this disability must fall in line with the guidelines set forth by the Americans with Disabilities Act. If, after this expensive testing is conducted, it is found that a disability does indeed exist, the individual will be granted accommodations. The two most common of these are extended time and preferential seating.

But what if we had a classroom where everyone could have their individual needs met without a piece of paper telling a teacher that it is okay to deviate from the norm? In my school, differentiation occurs every day for all students in a variety of ways. First, we do not have just two freshman English courses as many schools do. Most schools have the academic track and the honors track. Our school has five different courses available for freshman English, and this is not done via what would commonly be known as "tracking." What we do is review learning objectives for all our students, and we determine which students will need more focused attention on specific skills in specific areas of instruction. We place those students in classes that will differentiate to reinforce those needs. We then look at our students who may succeed best when there are more visual or kinesthetic opportunities for learning, and those students are placed accordingly.

We also have classes with pacing adjusted to fit the needs of those in the class, and the pace can either be accelerated or slowed down when necessary. A student who is better at math and science may be placed in classes that move at a faster pace for those subjects, and that same student may be placed in an English class that moves at a more moderate pace if his learning style supports that need. The majority of our classes also incorporate movement and/or visual presentation of information on a daily basis.

We also know that due to the kinesthetic nature of boys, they will do best if they do not have to sit in the same class for over an hour listening to lecture. Classes are scheduled for 45-minute blocks to allow for movement, which in turn stimulates brain activity. We also have a rotating schedule. Not everyone is a morning person. If a student who is not a morning person has math first period every day, this may lead to challenges that have nothing to do with the student's abilities. The challenges that may arise might have more to do with his lack of energy that early in the day. The rotating schedule allows the teachers to see students at different times of the day during the week.

We also allow students a choice in how they take notes, and some are allowed to record lectures while they type their notes while others prefer to write notes using pen and paper. We have a proven track record of success with our students, and their ability to succeed in college is improved tremendously by our willingness to work with individual needs rather than adhering to group averages when we make decisions regarding student needs.

THE IMPACT OF TECHNOLOGY

There are many forms of technology that can help to mitigate the effects of learning disabilities. In 1996, Michael Merzenich, Paula Tallal, Bill Jenkins, and Steve Miller formed a company called Scientific Learning. They created a computer program called *Fast ForWord*, which was designed to help language-impaired and learning-disabled children. The purpose of this program is to exercise all the basic brain functions involved in language. One important component of this program is a reward feature that will stimulate the release of dopamine that can help to reinforce patterns and consolidate map changes.

Studies have indicated that children who participate in this program make significant progress in speech, language, and auditory-processing tests and that they will maintain these gains for longer than six weeks after training occurs. Additionally, brain scans performed on children who participated in the training showed "increased activity in the left temporo-parietal cortex, and their scans began to show patterns that were similar to those of children who have no reading problems" (Doidge, 2007, p. 72). It is important to note that another study cited in an earlier chapter found the *Fast ForWord* did not demonstrate a statistically significant impact on comprehension for adolescent readers.

Third-party apps such as Notability can also aid students with learning disabilities. Notability provides students with the capability of recording lectures while simultaneously typing notes. The notes typed on the screen will sync to the recorded lecture, and a student may tap a word on the screen to move to that point in the lecture when replaying it. This information is delivered via both auditory and visual senses. According to Michu Kaku (2014) and Cathy Davidson (2011), information delivered while incorporating multiple senses is more likely to be committed to long-term memory. Therefore, the use of Notability could provide a valuable resource for students with learning disabilities.

These are just a few of the ways that technology can help to mitigate the effects of various learning disabilities. What is important to remember, however, is that there is a potential negative impact of technology on learning as well. Teenagers in particular are demonstrating that they have limited ability to maintain focus because of the constant distractions inherent in their technology. They can access games via the internet that they then share through instant messaging. Rather than focusing and paying attention to important lessons, they may spend time torn between the distraction of the messages and games that they receive and the lesson being learned. This is particularly true of unstructured homework time because it is often not monitored by adults, and it is also a time when teenagers want a break from school. This type of interrupted instruction will not lead to the type of learning necessary for college or for life after high school. This is something that adolescents must be taught, and the importance of focused attention for learning must be reinforced both at school and at home.

WHAT'S NEXT?

Michael Merzenich's theory of cognitive training is interesting and could help to inform the way that we deliver instruction in the future. In his 2004 Ted Talk, Merzenich describes what he terms as "the great epochs of brain plasticity." Merzenich indicates that the infant stage of brain development is the critical period when the brain sets up its basic processing machinery, and this is a period of dramatic change. Exposure to a repertoire of sounds will help to shape the brain at this phase of development. He sees the second great epoch of brain development as the time when the brain begins to refine its machinery as it masters a wide repertoire of skills and abilities. This phase occurs late in the 1st year of life and lasts until death. He believes that the brain can be trained to correct deficits because of this plasticity (Merzenich, 2014). This theory of brain plasticity indicated to me that perhaps technology could be used to affect comprehension if methods were consistent, purposeful, and both student- and teacher-directed.

As a researcher looking for ways to improve literacy outcomes for struggling readers, I determined that I would conduct my own study using existing (extant) data from Nelson-Denny Reading Test pre- and post-measures taken over a five-year period. Two years of that data was collected prior to the introduction of the iPad for literacy instruction, and three years of the data was collected after the iPad was introduced. The results, as they existed on paper, surprised me because the outcomes that I could observe were not matching up with the results of the standardized measure. In the coming chapters, I will discuss some of the causes of reading disabilities and provide research regarding the use of technology and other methods to mitigate the effects of these disabilities. I will also delve more deeply into the background, methods, and the results of this study, which is one of the few that has sought to measure the impact of iPad multimodalities on literacy for adolescent males.

CHAPTER 7

21ST CENTURY LITERACY

According to noted literacy expert Maryanne Wolf, who established The Center for Reading and Language Research at Tuft's University, there is a noticeable change in students' reading comprehension capabilities when reading from screen-based technology. Dr. Wolf asserts that because students are now conditioned to read from screens, they have become conditioned to skimming and scanning for information. One unfortunate result of this is that students often do not see reading as a process that requires specific focus, and as a result, they are less likely to connect their reading to prior knowledge. This is a crucial step towards comprehension because deep-level reading skills are not activated when information is simply skimmed over. When surface-level reading skills are the primary focus of the reading process, very little is retained. These surface-level skills focus mainly on decoding and not on vocabulary attainment or true comprehension. This type of reading does not lead to the type of analysis and synthesis that promote true learning (Learning Disabilities Association of America, April 2001).

Wolf, who is the author of *Our Deep Reading Brain: Its Digital Evolution Poses Questions* (2010), suggested that the way that we read information may have as much of an impact on comprehension as the content of what we read does. As mentioned previously, reading print-based books using traditional linear reading practices encourages readers to connect information sequentially and to anticipate outcomes. Dr. Wolf's research supports the need for early reading instruction that encourages the development of linear reading practices before moving students

The Rise of the Human Digital Brain:
How Multidirectional Thinking is Changing the Way We Learn, pages 61–72.

to digital reading practices. Once the linear reading practices have been firmly established, a move to digital reading will be more successful.

This also supports the Learning Disabilities Association's belief that intensive teaching of reading, written language, and spelling in elementary and secondary school is crucial to establishing the necessary building blocks for literacy. As more and more schools move towards classroom use of digital devices as a primary mode of instruction, some of these important linear processes are being lost. Spelling is no longer emphasized because it is assumed that technology can address spelling concerns. What is not considered is the fact that the measures for success in college, such as the ACT or the SAT, are not taken via electronic means for most students. Therefore, a student who lacks adequate spelling skills may score lower on a standardized measure.

Education, as it existed through the 19th and 20th centuries, often included the type of rote memorization (to include learning how to spell words) that was designed to strengthen auditory memory. A strong focus on handwriting, which has almost disappeared from 21st century schools, also existed, and this helped to strengthen motor capacities which in turn added speed and fluency to reading and speaking abilities (Doidge, 2007). According to Dr. Norman Doidge, author of the New York Times bestseller *The Brain That Changes Itself: Stories of Personal Triumph from the Frontiers of Brain Science*, the loss of this type of "drill and kill" has been costly to 21st century students. These students are losing out on the opportunity to exercise the brain functions that promote "fluency and grace with symbols" (p. 42).

READING DISABILITIES

Developmental dyslexia is defined as "A severe difficulty with the written form of language independent of intellectual, cultural, and emotional causation. The difficulty is a cognitive one affecting those language skills associated with the written form, particularly visual, verbal coding, short-term memory, order perception, and sequencing" (Price, 2006, p. 22). In an article published in 2013 in the *Journal of Research in Special Education Needs*, the authors state that people read at a speed that allows them to maintain meaning and understanding, and when a reading disability such as dyslexia impedes this process, it can have a significant impact on reading comprehension (Reid et al., 2013). Some studies estimate that at as much as 20% of the population have reading disabilities; however, only about 4% of school-age students will receive special education services for reading disabilities (Shaywitz, 2003). These learning disabilities may result from neurological variances. Some struggling readers demonstrate adequate decoding skills but lack skills associated with comprehension. Other struggling readers have difficulty decoding information, but they demonstrate adequate comprehension skills when things are read aloud to them. Both problems lead to lack of fluency.

According to neuroscientist Michael Merzenich, a learning disability related to language (such as reading) occurs when the language processing center of the brain is created in a "defective form." He explains that early in the brain's life if the "machine process" is noisy, this creates a signal to noise problem. Because the auditory process is so important in brain development, something such as frequent ear infections for an infant or even constant exposure to a noisy fan can interfere with the brain's ability to process language. According to Merzenich, if the problem is addressed early in the brain's development, the disorder can be corrected. He refers to "muffled language" and the fact that it creates an unclear mental representation. Language is degraded when hearing is interrupted, and this results in a defective representation of words and sounds. This may create memory and cognitive deficits that will result in poor reading skills later in life (Merzenich, 2004).

Dr. Merzenich refers to "brain maps" in order to help us understand how learning occurs. According to Merzenich, brain-processing power is allocated selectively. The brain creates certain maps, and each of these maps competes for resources to sustain themselves. The term "use it or lose it" applies to the brain's need for reinforcement of skills for them to remain accessible. This leads to the theory of competitive plasticity, which refers to "an endless war of nerves going on inside each of our brains. If we stop exercising our mental skills, we do not just forget them: the brain map space for those skills is turned over to the skills we practice instead" (Doidge, 2007, p. 59). Competitive plasticity can also help us to understand why *when* children learn to read is just as important as *how* they learn to read. Because it is so much harder to unlearn bad habits later in life, it is also very important that good habits be established early (Doidge, 2007). A child who learns good reading habits early in life will not be forced to relearn these processes later while simultaneously attempting to unlearn established bad habits.

According to Merzenich, brain maps are organized topographically, and this is done for efficiency. For example, the parts of the brain that often work together are close in proximity within the brain so that signals do not have to travel as far, thus conserving mental energy. This order emerged because many of our daily activities are so rote and occur in repeated patterns. As we repeat these patterns again and again, neurons fire, and "neurons that fire together wire together" (Doidge, 2007, p. 65). Reading is a process that eventually results in automaticity (or becomes automatic) after it is practiced appropriately over a period of time, yet 5 to 10% of preschool children already have established language disabilities by the time that they enter school that will make learning to read difficult for them (Doidge, 2007).

Paula Tallal, a researcher at Rutgers University, analyzed why children have difficulty reading. Her research showed that children with language disabilities often have auditory processing problems with certain consonant-vowel combinations. Children who have difficulty hearing these sounds accurately will reproduce them inaccurately. After reviewing Tallal's research, Dr. Merzenich hypothesized that children with language difficulties had auditory cortex neurons that were firing too slowly, and this inhibited their ability to distinguish the difference between two similar sounds. Merzenich believed that improper hearing would lead to weakness in all language tasks, to include vocabulary, comprehension, speech, reading, and writing. Additionally, so much energy was being used to decode words that these children often used shorter sentences, thus taxing their memories less and leading to working and long-term memory deficiencies (Doidge, 2007).

A 2006 study of dyslexic students in higher education focused on learning technology available for readers diagnosed with dyslexia. This study followed three dyslexic college students to see how they used different types of software to overcome writing anxiety, fear of the blank page syndrome, and issues of plagiarism. The study found that mind-mapping software helped to support individual cognitive styles and that talking spell checkers and thesauruses helped students with dyslexia to bypass weak visual-memory skills. The researcher also found that colored acetates and individualized screen color backgrounds could reduce the visual distress that a dyslexic reader may experience (Price, 2006).

NATIONAL READING PANEL REPORT ON LITERACY

In an attempt to further analyze the causes of and potential fixes for literacy deficiencies in school-age children, Congress asked the Director of the National Institute of Child Health and Human Development, in consultation with the Secretary of Education, to convene a national panel of 14 individuals, including leading scientists in reading research, representatives from universities, reading teachers, educational administrators, and parents, to explore the existing research regarding approaches to teaching reading and the effectiveness of various methods. This report, entitled *Teaching Children to Read: An Evidence-Based Assessment of the Scientific Research Literature on Reading and its Implications for Reading Instruction* (2000), was quite extensive, starting with over 100,000 studies and eventually being narrowed down to only those that met certain established criteria, such as a review of outcome measures, sufficient detail of study interventions to allow for replication, and specific descriptions of study participants.

The results of the report, which was initiated in 1997, were made available to Congress in 2000. This was the last major meta-analysis conducted in the United States with the express purpose of determining best practices for mitigating literacy deficits. Think about all the technology that has become available since the year 2000. We have yet to conduct a major meta-analysis of research regarding the use of modern technology to affect literacy outcomes. In part, this is because technology moves so quickly that it is difficult to conduct a study and publish results before the technology has again changed. Whatever the reason, it should be a priority in the field of education to understand how technology is (and potentially could be) affecting literacy attainment and educational outcomes. We need to be searching for ways to mitigate these often life-altering gaps in education that may lead to a lack of skills necessary to gain future employment.

COMMON INTERVENTIONS FOR READING DISABILITIES

It is common practice in schools across the country to adopt a single method for teaching reading. This usually focuses on surface-level reading skills, such as decoding and phonemic awareness, but not all students learn the same way. The Learning Disabilities Association of America (LDA) stresses that no single reading method will be effective for all students with learning disabilities. In 1996, the LDA expressed (and continues to believe) that illiteracy is a national crisis and that to affect a significant increase in reading achievement for all, there are several elements that must be in place:

- A variety of methods for teaching reading in schools (in regular and special education) and in adult literacy programs
- Intensive teaching of reading, written language, and spelling in elementary and secondary school
- Screening and diagnostic programs to identify students with reading disabilities
- Evaluation of program effectiveness that goes beyond mandated periodic testing
- Teacher certification requirements for elementary, secondary and special education teachers include substantive courses in reading methodologies
- Individualized reading programs for students with learning disabilities
- A strong commitment to research which will identify causes/prevention of reading failure and effective interventions (Learning Disabilities Association of America, April 2001)

According to the 2000 National Reading Panel Report, 20% of elementary school students are at risk for reading failure and 5-10% will have difficulty learning to read using methods that work for most students. This is one reason why technology can be a strong leverage point for 21st century learners. The type of technology that is available to students today can be individualized. Accommodations that do not follow the "one size fits all" model indeed do appear to be the type that can be used to improve outcomes for students across the country, but how do we successfully use technology as a leverage point in 21st century classrooms?

TECHNOLOGY AND LITERACY

Even though we have entered the "Age of the Internet," linear processes are still the primary mode of obtaining information. This may be a positive thing in grade schools, as the use of traditional linear methods can help to establish and reinforce strong surface-level and deep-level reading skills for most students. However, if technology is to be used effectively as a tool to mitigate literacy deficits, these linear patterns of thought should be firmly established prior to its introduction.

When technology is introduced too early, it can create a disruption in the acquisition of the skills necessary for comprehension. This occurs because the digital-reading brain is more multidirectional in pattern, and if a student has not yet been taught how to explicitly connect information sequentially and activate prior knowledge effectively, true comprehension will not occur. For example, to read information from an iPad, Kindle, or other form of tablet technology, users look up, down, sideways and across as they access links or use additional functions available on tablet technology. We now know, thanks to brain imaging technology, that the pattern for reading is not set in a linear fashion as it has been for centuries, and this is probably due in large part to the introduction of technology as a medium for reading. This can create a disconnect when we expect students to apply linear processes to reading, yet they have not clearly established those patterns in their reading behaviors because they primarily read via digital mediums.

Because certain forms of technology, such as iPhones and iPads, have now become common fixtures in American culture, a great deal of reading is done via these types of tablet technologies. Despite the disruption to linear processes caused by the introduction of these tablet technologies, some positive attributes also exist. Tablet-based technologies provide multimodal learning opportunities that may be used to assist readers with decoding deficits or processing delays. They can also be used to mitigate long-term memory deficits through the variety of apps that provide opportunities to manipulate information in a variety of ways through different sensory opportunities. However, there is still little information that exists to accurately measure the impact of this new technology on reading comprehension and vocabulary attainment, but (given the right conditions) the potential is promising.

As noted in earlier chapters, Brain-Based Learning Theory indicates that "through experience and physical activities, students can strengthen the synoptic links between neurons. Experiences physically change the brain through internal and external stimuli" (Duman, 2010, p. 2081). As a result, learning occurs through experience, and different teaching styles must be used to meet different learning objectives. A variety of tools are available through the multimodalities of the iPad. Changing the modes of instruction and assessment to meet the changing brain structures and patterns reinforced by the constant presence of technology in the world (and now in the classroom) could provide tremendous benefits to students (Davidson, 2011; Duman, 2010; Gardner & Davis, 2013; Kaku, 2014). We must keep in mind, however, that the timing of the introduction of technology can also impact its success as a tool for literacy attainment. According to Michael Gurian, that time should not be prior to the time that a child reaches 14 years of age. This is probably because young, developing brains need time to establish important linear patterns before being introduced to the multidirectional patterns that are reinforced by many forms of technology.

The iPad. The multimodal and web-based interactive technology that is available via the iPad became more accessible as a learning tool in American classrooms in 2012 (Reid et al., 2013). The iPad has many capabilities that have the potential to assist students with specific reading disabilities such as dyslexia. Students with dyslexia need for tasks to be differentiated, structured, clarified, and focused toward a child's stronger area of learning. The multimodalities of the iPad offer differentiated instruction that can be tailored to the needs of individual learners (Reid et al., 2013).

To assist with visual and verbal coding differences, the iPad offers a variety of fonts that may be more visually discernible for an individual with dyslexia. There are also dyslexic types that may be easily downloaded into Word or Pages to increase readability for students with dyslexia. Additionally, iPad users can change background colors (Cheung & Slavin, 2014; Price, 2006). As noted earlier, Larson's 2012 report indicated that all these capabilities were shown to improve reading fluency for students with dyslexia or other diagnosed reading disabilities. There was little to no impact on comprehension demonstrated, however. So while the use of the iPad for literacy instruction may impact surface-level reading skills, it did not impact the deeper-level reading skills that could lead to greater comprehension. This points to a need for stronger vocabulary building efforts in conjunction with fluency exercises when teaching early reading skills.

Another capability available to users of the iPad that seems to aid in fluency is the text-to-speech (TTS) feature. Nancy Meyer and Emily Bouck conducted a 2014 study of three students who were struggling readers with varied learning differences. This study measured the effectiveness of text-to-speech software on reading fluency and comprehension for struggling readers. Although the findings did not show a significant boost in skill, the social validity aspect of the experiment indicated that the students believed they were able to read more quickly and that TTS had an impact on their fluency.

In a 2015 update of the IOS system, a two-finger swipe was introduced to the capabilities of the iPad. Users may simply use two fingers to swipe down from the top of the iPad screen to produce a menu that will provide the option of text-to-voice capabilities. Individuals who use this feature can access written information simultaneously through both visual and auditory senses. As noted earlier, studies indicate that the more senses involved in the learning process, the more likely that information is to be stored in the long-term memory (Davidson, 2011; Kaku, 2014).

Apps. iPads have the capability to download apps, and some have likened these apps to a "digital education prescription pad" (Reid et al., 2013, p. 175) because of their ability to instantly provide individualized accommodations for all students, particularly those with reading disabilities. Many of these apps can help a student who struggles with decoding and fluency. Research conducted by Don McMahon, a professor in the College of Education at Washington State University, on the impact of iPads and other IOS devices on reading fluency identified some of the apps that can allow students to process using both auditory and visual means. The apps included in the study were AudioNote, which allows students to record lectures and take notes at the same time; the Dragon Dictation app, which has a free version, allows students to convert speech to text; and Garage Band, which allows teachers to create podcasts that a dyslexic student may listen to through earphones during tests so that the questions may be read aloud to the student without disturbing other students in the classroom. Although these apps had an impact on access to information, there was not enough data to suggest a definite positive impact on comprehension and fluency (McMahon, 2014).

A 2014 article by Benjamin Herold entitled "Digital Reading Poses Learning Challenges for Students" details an attempt to study the effectiveness of apps that were created to enhance comprehension, including Curriculet, Actively Learn, and Sub-Text. Each of these apps has a limited free version available, and they also have paid versions that offer more options and capabilities. These apps focus on providing increased engagement with the text using imbedded videos, teacher generated questions, and dictionaries (Herold, 2014). The main purpose of these apps is to encourage struggling or reluctant readers to stop, take a moment to revisit a concept, and then proceed to read with a deeper understanding of the text. Although the study hoped to find a significant difference in comprehension for students using these apps, the study concluded that while the apps increased student interest, they did not have a statistically-significant impact on comprehension.

Due to the expense of this type of technology, there are still many educational settings that are unable to provide access to students, but exposure is growing every year. As previously mentioned, there is also a lack of credible studies regarding the long-term effects of such technology on reading comprehension and fluency due to the rapidly changing nature and modes of the technology available. This lack of information regarding web-based interactive technology and multimodal digital texts on literacy has made it difficult to ascertain whether this type of technology can be used to reduce the trends of lower literacy rates, particularly among male adolescent readers (Gardner & Davis, 2013).

Other mobile technologies. Paul Conway and Jessica Amerson conducted a 2011 study concerning the impact of laptops on learning that divided laptops into three models: fixed, floating, and fostered. The fixed model had students working collaboratively in a learning community and sharing their work on a laptop kept in one location; the floating model had students taking ownership and responsibility for the equipment and their learning, and laptops were used on an as needed basis; and the fostered model had students using a designating a laptop. The fostered laptop model allowed for students to use the laptop both at home and at school. The study found that laptops "Fitted into rather than transformed provisions for students with dyslexia and other reading difficulties" (p. 179). Laptop-enhanced literacy learning did, however, provide more learning opportunities for students with literacy difficulties.

Researchers from The College at Brockport: State University of New York conducted a study in 2013 regarding how reading behaviors change with the medium. The study focused on three groups with 30 participants in each (23 males and 67 females) with an age range from 18 to 25. None of the participants had diagnosed learning disabilities, and their reading behaviors were evaluated using a questionnaire. The participants were tested using five expository passages and five narrative passages. The reading passages were presented in three different mediums: paper, computer, and Kindle.

The results of the study indicated that there was no significant difference in comprehension for students using the different mediums of paper, computer, or Kindle, but working memory, the most important factor for comprehension, was affected. When students accessed hyperlinks or highlighted information to have it read to them, a distraction that interfered with the process of working memory occurred. This had a slightly negative impact on reading fluency, and it may also have interfered with comprehension.

In a 2013 study published in the *Journal of Research in Reading*, direct-reading strategy instruction was compared to computer-based guided practice. In this study, nine 6th-grade classes of 148 students were followed over the course of one school year. This was a randomly selected group, but the students selected were recruited from the lower-performing third of students within the regular school system. The students were broken into two groups, and each group was taught using different methods. The program Reading Detective involved a teacher-directed instruction of metacognitive knowledge, while the other program, conText, involved a computer-assisted and content-focused intervention with a guided practice approach. Results were collected using pre- and post-tests conducted during four- and eight-week intervals. The results indicated that there were no significant differences in comprehension and only slightly higher trends toward higher performance in verbal intelligence and fluency in the conText group (Lenhard, 2013).

A study published in 2013 in the *Journal of Educational Technology & Society* sought to determine if e-readers and internet resources could support and increase comprehension of students with no diagnosed or discernible reading disabilities. In this research, the word "digital natives" is used to refer to children who were born into a world of electronic mediums in which their brains are immediately wired to acknowledge electronically operated devices. The study focused on three second-grade female students who were asked to read two paper-based books and two e-books. As the girls read paper-based books, they were given access to hard copies of resources such as dictionaries and thesauruses. When the girls read e-books, they had electronic access to definitions of words simply by touching the word on the screen, and they also had similar access to an electronic thesaurus. Their findings indicated that vocabulary and reading comprehension was consistent between the two mediums; however, students were found to be more likely to utilize reading resources (such as the thesaurus or dictionary) when engaged in digital text. Additionally, students were found to take longer to complete reading when engaged in an e-book, but they reported greater enjoyment of the reading experience (Wright et al., 2013).

COMMON CORE STANDARDS

In a 2011 article in the *Journal of Adolescent and Adult Literature*, the authors noted that "to be literate today means being able to use some combination of blogs, wikis, texts, search engines, Facebook, Foursquare, Google Docs, Skype, etc., including thousands of apps," (Leu et al., 2011, p. 6). To successfully use technology to impact learning, 21st century educators must become familiar enough with its various forms. The standards in countries like Australia are already changing to reflect digital literacy requirements.

In 2009, the United States also sought to establish more uniform standards across the states (referred to as the Common Core) to prepare students for college and careers in the 21st century. These standards, which were developed with the input of educators, standards experts, education agency leaders, and established feedback groups, were distributed to states in 2010, the same year that the iPad was released. As of 2017, only one of the anchor standards of the Common Core pertains to internet literacy. This standard is one of the English Language Arts Standards, and it pertains to the strategic and capable use of technology and digital media (Common Core Standards Initiative, 2010). Forty-two states and all Department of Defense Education Activity (DoDEA) schools have adopted these standards. These standards have yet to be updated since their 2010 release, even though technology has changed tremendously over the past 7 years.

In 2010, when the Common Core was established, one of the primary uses of technology in the classroom was its application as a search engine. Students would search for information, scan the results, and skim the articles for specific answers. When students are asked to read for meaning using a digital medium, they often associate this with those types of surface-level internet searches.

In a 2012 article entitled "It's Time to Turn the Digital Page: Pre-Service Teachers Explore e-Book Reading," Dr. Lotta C. Larson points out the fact that teachers must also be prepared to teach students how to read for meaning on mobile devices. This may be difficult given the fact that students are more apt to "skim and scan" when reading e-texts because this is the same method that they apply when reading anything via mobile devices.

In a related 2013 study entitled "Investigating Synergies Between Literacy, Technology, and Classroom Practice," the researchers found that teachers felt pressured to use technology in their classrooms. The teachers in this study indicated that they found little time to prepare appropriate lessons. They also indicated that they had limited time and training to develop their own digital literacy skills before being tasked with teaching those skills to their students (Kervin, Verenikina, & Jones et al., 2013). This can have a direct impact on the effectiveness of the technology being used. As teachers abandon familiar methods that have proven effective in the past, they often begin using new methods that they may not have as much skill with as the students in front of them do.

LACK OF FLUENCY RESULTING FROM POOR DECODING AND WORD ATTACK SKILLS

In a 2013 article published in the *Journal of Reading Research,* Wolfgang Lenhard states that "meta-analyses implicate phonemic awareness, phonics, fluency, vocabulary and comprehension programs as central approaches in literacy education" (p. 224). The National Reading Panel also noted these findings in 2000 (as cited in Cheung & Slavin, 2014). The simultaneous use of all five of the skills listed above allows fluency and comprehension to take place. Successful readers will develop these skills in the primary grades, but struggling readers may fail for a variety of reasons.

While the skills of phonemic awareness, phonics, fluency, vocabulary, and comprehension are central to literacy education, a sixth important yet often overlooked skill is visualization, which is considered a deep-level reading strategy. As noted in previous chapters, visualizations are like "movies of the mind," and they are used to create mental images and to envision situations. Visualization reveals the different lenses used to interpret and understand what is being read. These lenses can "illuminate, clarify, and magnify the meaning of words or text, and they can also distort, exclude, and confirm stereotypes" (Park, 2012, p. 633). A disruption to the acquisition of any of the skills listed above may lead to lack of adequate skills necessary for vocabulary and comprehension attainment.

CONSTRAINED AND UNCONSTRAINED READING SKILLS

In a 2005 article in *Reading Research* Quarterly, Scott Paris referred to the process of reading as a series of constrained and unconstrained reading skills. Constrained reading skills would refer to those that have boundaries or limits. The fact that there are a finite number of letter combinations to represent sounds means that there is a limit to the rate of reading that may be sustained without a sacrifice of accuracy and meaning. The skills that are more easily measured are phonemic awareness, alphabetics, phonics, and fluency, which are all considered constrained reading skills. The skills of vocabulary and comprehension, on the other hand, are unconstrained reading skills.

Unconstrained reading skills exhibit no endpoint because vocabulary and reading comprehension may continue to increase through practice (Fisher, Frey, & Hattie, 2016). Fluency is increased through continued practice, but it is also impeded if the proper constrained skills are not effectively taught as lack of knowledge of phonemes and alphabetics will lead to deficits in decoding skills. Constrained reading skills would be deemed surface-level reading strategies, yet they are critical. Reading instruction that is most effective will involve both constrained and unconstrained reading skills.

REPEATED READING

A 2010 literature review on the efficacy of repeated reading and wide reading practice interventions for high school students with severe reading disabilities had interesting results. Repeated reading is a "method of instruction where a student listens to a passage as it is read by a teacher and then reads the same passage to himself or herself before finally reading it aloud. Rate, accuracy and prosody are calculated and reported to the students with the goal being an increase in all three with subsequent attempts" (Fisher et al., 2016, p. 63). The researchers cited a meta-analysis of 19 studies focused on effective practices to increase struggling secondary school readers' fluency. The results demonstrated that reading rate outcomes could consistently be improved using repeated reading interventions such as listening to an audiotape or an adult model of good reading before reading the text or providing corrective feedback. This improvement in fluency did not necessarily equate to an improvement in comprehension, however (Wexler, Vaughn, Roberts, & Denton, 2010).

CRITICAL-PERIOD PLASTICITY

David Hubel and Torsten Wiesel won the Nobel Prize in 1981 for their work in the field of neuroplasticity. They found that in certain instances, the brain can rewire itself to regain critical functions that have been lost due to injury or disability. They determined that the brain has a "critical period" of plasticity, which indicates that each neural system has a window of time when it will remain "especially plastic and sensitive to the environment," thus leading to rapid, formative growth. According to these findings, "language has a critical period of development that begins in infancy and ends between 8 years of age and puberty" (Doidge, 2007, p. 52). Armed with this information, literacy teachers should now be able to leverage this critical-period of plasticity to help students learn how to read effectively as well as to help those with reading disabilities mitigate the effects of those disabilities. With this research in hand, the possibilities appear limitless if the information is shared and used effectively.

CHAPTER 8

TEACHING IN THE DIGITAL AGE

The 21st Century Model for Literacy Instruction

You see it everywhere you go these days—people glued to their iPhones or other digital devices and failing to interact with or even notice those around them. This is particularly true of teenagers, most of whom have yet to develop the type of self-regulation skills necessary to be able to turn away from their digital devices for even a few moments. According to Tristan Harris, former Silicon Valley engineer and Google product manager, this is the very deliberate result of a tech world that is engaging in something being referred to as "brain hacking." Harris explains that "brain hacking" is akin to turning the brain into a slot machine. Every time you check your device, there is a hope that some type of positive response will be received. A positive response will result in the release of dopamine in the brain, which can create a momentary feeling of euphoria. According to Harris, we have become so addicted to our iPhones and electronic devices that we are left with only two options: be left out or be a part of the action. He feels that the element of choice has been diminished (Harris, 2016). The bigger question here is what happens when this type of technology crosses into our work world or, worse yet, into the world of education for young children and teens?

When I first introduced the iPad into my classroom in 2012, I was excited about the possibilities that might emerge with the addition of this multimodal

The Rise of the Human Digital Brain:
How Multidirectional Thinking is Changing the Way We Learn, pages 73–82.

technology that had never before been available in classrooms. Dyslexic students would now be able to alter the color of the screens or the shape of the fonts in order to more clearly decode information. Better yet, there were opportunities for them to hear text being read aloud. Students with dysgraphia would be able to dictate information directly into the iPad and never have to type a word. Students who were strong visual learners could be exposed to vocabulary lists with images attached to help them remember the meaning of words. It appeared to be a teacher's dream—and then reality set in.

THE FIRST YEAR

As I contemplated how to best shape instruction now that the iPad was available to all my students, I recalled what I had learned in my education courses about the function of systems. A system, as defined by noted System's Theory expert Donatella Meadows (2008), is an "interconnected set of elements that is coherently organized in a way that achieves something" (p. 1). All systems have a purpose, and all have leverage points. In the case of my reading class, the purpose was to create stronger readers. The iPad could be used as a leverage point in that it provided a variety of ways to mitigate learning differences. For example, a student who struggled with decoding and was a very auditory learner would be able to by-pass the decoding difficulties (which are surface-level skills) and move into the deeper-level reading skills required for comprehension. The Figure 8.1 chart demonstrates this:

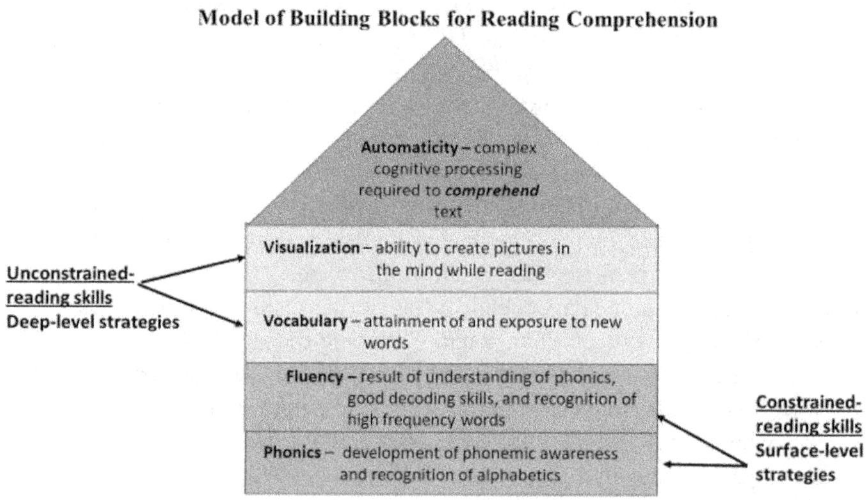

FIGURE 8.1. Building Blocks for Reading Comprehension. (Adapted from the 2000 National Reading Panel Report on Teaching Children to Read and research from Park (2012) Using Visualizing to Bride Reading Comprehension and Critical Literacy.

As the chart indicates, surface-level reading strategies are necessary for comprehension to occur, but they are constrained skills, which (as noted earlier) means that there are only so many that must be learned before meaning is derived. To develop adequate decoding and fluency skills, there are a restricted number of letters and sounds to learn. This differs from unconstrained skills where there are an infinite number of new, more complex words to learn and a multitude of ways to understand complex texts. When a child misses the opportunity to effectively develop the constrained, surface-level skills of decoding and fluency, he is, for lack of a better term, "stuck" and unable to move into the unconstrained reading skills. Deep-level reading that leads to comprehension and automaticity (developing a skill to the point that it happens automatically) will not occur if a child is stuck trying to master surface-level skills. Technology can allow a student to bypass the bottom two surface-level skills and move right into the deep-level reading strategies (Fisher et al., 2016).

I determined that the key to promoting stronger literacy skills would be to develop a system that would make maximum use of the leverage points provided by technology. I reviewed my teaching methods and studied the differences between reading books in the traditional paper format and reading books in a digital format. I found that the digital format would offer opportunities for active note taking that was not available with traditional books issued from the school library. As we began to read our first book in digital format, I painstakingly demonstrated to my students how to take effective notes and how to highlight information using the available functions of iBooks. I also showed them how to search for information in a digital book and how to use the search feature to pinpoint certain notes they sought to access. I shared with them ways to change the font of the type and the background color of the screens, and I also encouraged the use of headphones or earbuds so that students could listen as they read along with the text. I thought that certainly this would add to comprehension skills.

As we progressed through our first iBook, I noticed that my students began demonstrating higher-order thinking skills by asking questions aimed at analysis, and they were no longer confined to questions focused on basic knowledge of facts. More importantly, they were making connections to other things in the world because of what they read. They were demonstrating the ability to synthesize information. They posted questions on electronic information boards regarding the reading, and they researched and posted answers to those questions. The students then applied those answers to their own experiences by posting reflection papers. Many of them went beyond expectations by finding links to videos and articles that pertained to their reading and posting and sharing those with each other. This led to engaging discussions that encouraged students to continue to seek out new information in a variety of forms. For students who had demonstrated poor reading progress for the first nine years of their educational experience, this was a noteworthy breakthrough. I was certain that real progress had been made.

When the year was over, I administered the traditional Nelson-Denny Reading Test (NDRT) to measure progress in comprehension and vocabulary attainment. After recording the scores, I compared both the vocabulary and comprehension NDRT scores from the first year of iPad use to the two years prior to the introduction of the iPad. The vocabulary scores were positive, and similar gains were exhibited between the two groups. However, as noted in chapter 10 where the results of this study are found, I discovered that growth in comprehension had dropped by nearly half! As I sought to determine why, I began to realize two important things: first, the Nelson-Denny Comprehension Test that I had given to the students measured mostly linear thought processes, and my students were not learning in traditional, linear patterns; second, the many "distractions" embedded in the technology that was being used while reading appeared to be impacting linear thinking. The very thing that could aid many of these students by streamlining instruction and increasing comprehension and retention of information while simultaneously promoting creativity was also reinforcing a new type of thinking and learning.

THE DANCE OF DISTRACTION

As the iPad one-to-one initiative unfolded at my school, the need for the development of self-regulation skills obviously emerged as an important focal point. The school put restrictions in place to aid students in good decision making. Students were only allowed to play games during lunch, and they were to self-regulate and avoid using the games during the rest of the school day. In the classrooms, teachers, who had no real previous experience with this type of technology, were left to monitor the screens of all students in front of them. It was a learn as you go situation for all involved. Some of these savvy students quickly figured out that busy teachers could not always tell what they were doing on their screens, and so began the dance of distraction.

Many students realized that the addition of the iPad to the classroom increased the potential for multitasking, and while this is not always a bad thing, in many instances it can be detrimental to the learning process. Dr. Michael Merzenich, expert in brain plasticity, notes that while we can learn when we divide our attention, "divided attention doesn't lead to abiding change in your brain maps," (Doidge, 2007, p. 68). In other words, the very type of attention that is necessary to understand a new concept being taught in school is inhibited when a student is taken off task by distractions.

Gloria Mark, Professor in the Department of Informatics at the University of California, Irvine, completed a study that supports this belief. Dr. Mark had observers go into the workplace to time people's activities. She found that 82% of all interrupted work is resumed on the same day, but it takes an average of 23 minutes and 15 seconds to get back to the original task. Something as simple as checking a score update can take 23 minutes of time away from an individual's focus on the task at hand! (Berman, 2003). Additionally, the access to not only information but also to games, instant messaging, updates, and a multitude of other things that are embedded in iPad functions can be distracting and may potentially cause us to lose ground in traditionally linear tasks.

My concern began to grow as I realized the disruptive nature of the distractions inherent in this type of technology. Because most of us have experience with this type of technology outside of the classroom (through our iPhones), iPads are already viewed not as mere learning tools, as perhaps a calculator may be, but they are viewed as all-in-one devices where entertainment and educational tools comingle without any perceived repercussions. Because these devices were created with both the potential to be an educational platform as well as an entertainment platform, it is difficult to separate one from the other. I began to realize that the distracting nature of even the mere thought of access to entertainment was enough to render the iPads less effective as a viable means of instruction for many students. The danger that was overlooked was what those distractions would do to a student's ability to concentrate.

Fortunately, my school provides a very disciplined environment and quickly realized the potential distractions inherent in these devices. As a result, additional restrictions were put in place and consistent monitoring is now standard. As I speak with educators in different schools and different systems (both public and private) across the country, I am hearing that the same concerns are being observed in virtually all settings. This is by no means an isolated problem, and it will continue to be observed in various forms as long as students are introduced to technology at earlier and earlier ages. This is a system-wide problem, yet it cannot be controlled by changes to the system alone. We must be willing to realize the social interactions and exposures that are driving the changes in our students and how they think and learn.

As noted earlier, thanks to recent brain imaging, we now know that iPads, smartphones, and Xboxes act on the brain much in the same way that certain drugs do. This brain imaging demonstrates that the frontal cortex, which controls executive functioning, is affected by technology much in the same way it is affected by cocaine. Studies also show that too much screen time increases anxiety, depression, and aggression (Kardaras, 2016). To fully process the effect that technology was having on children, and particularly adolescents, I took some time to reflect back on some successful methods I had used in the past when I taught students who were used to traditional linear methods of instruction.

ACTIVE AND DYNAMIC TEACHING

In 2002, I was hired to teach at a Department of Defense high school, and I was informed that my senior English class would be required to read Mary Shelley's *Frankenstein.* I had never taught this particular novel before, so one of my kind colleagues who had been teaching the piece for several years provided me with copies of her tests and quizzes. Most of them had been copied from pre-packaged teaching units sold to schools in the 1980s and 1990s. I was relieved that I would not have to "recreate the wheel," and I eagerly began to review the contents of the binder provided and prepared to engage with material designed to make high school seniors understand, love, and appreciate Shelley's classic work.

As I opened the binder, I found material that was surprisingly familiar in content and form. The multiple choice and true and false format had been common during my high school years, and they were certainly designed to reinforce the lower-order thinking skills of knowledge and comprehension. They did not, however, go much further than that. One of the multiple-choice questions included in the material provided to me read as follows:

Whom did the creature save?

a. A woman separated from her friends
b. A mountain climber who had fallen
c. A shepherd and his flock from an attack
d. A girl from drowning

This question was designed to demonstrate knowledge of the events in the book, but it also asked a question that could be easily answered without reading the book and by simply reviewing *Spark Notes*. It did not require that this information be connected to prior knowledge to formulate new ideas. In other words, this question does not require the individual to think. Another question in this packet read as follows:

> **True or False**: The creature was delighted that he was able to create despair for his creator.

While this appears to be a question that may cause the reader to make inferences about the feelings of the creature, it is actually another question at the lowest level of Bloom's Taxonomy. The creature clearly states in the novel that he is elated to see his creator suffer like he did. It is another question that can be answered based simply on basic knowledge of the story.

I decided to attempt to rewrite the tests in order to engage students by requiring that they use the higher-order thinking skills of analysis and synthesis. Rather than asking whom the creature saved, I rewrote the question as follows:

- Analyze the creature's actions in chapters 16–20 and, in a well-developed paragraph that includes specific examples from the story, explain the following:
- Whom did the creature save and why did he choose to save this individual?
- What causes the creature to seize the small boy and why, in your opinion, does he harm the boy?
- Do you feel that the creature is justified in this act? Why or why not?

This level of questioning was more individualized and required more engagement with the material for a student to be able to provide an effective answer.

As the students began reading the novel, we created discussion groups centered around genetic engineering. This allowed a level of analysis and synthesis to occur that was absent from the standard and rote methods previously used. Students became actively engaged with the material as they staged debates to support their positions. They directly interacted with the text as they used examples from it to support their positions either for or against genetic engineering.

We also read Arthur Miller's play *The Crucible*. To promote active engagement with the text, we stopped in the middle of the play and staged our own trial. Students were assigned roles and had to actively engage in research beyond the information provided in the text to accurately portray their assigned characters. A defense team and a prosecutorial team were then established, and a judge was appointed. After the trial was over, the class read the rest of the play and then, for the final test, students analyzed their results and compared them to those revealed in the conclusion of the trial in the play. From there, we discussed McCarthyism, and the students looked for examples of modern day witch hunts. Presentations were created, and education became an engaging process as parallels to the text and real life were drawn.

When my freshmen were assigned to read William Shakespeare's *Romeo and Juliet*, we turned the entire classroom into the Globe Theatre. Every student was tasked with researching one aspect of the Globe, and once all the information had been gathered, the students worked together to create a representation of The Globe Theatre in our classroom. Students earned pennies during lessons for answering questions about the play correctly, and these pennies could be spent on performance day when root beer and peanuts would be available for purchase. Students were even allowed to throw peanut shells on the floor as was done in the actual Globe Theatre (they did also clean up after themselves!). Soon, our classroom was transformed into the Globe, and one act of the play was reenacted. The students were excited about learning, and this translated into a genuine interest in the material and a better understanding of the time period in which it was written. Test grades also demonstrated how much making students active participants in the process aided in their retention of material.

When my seniors read *Beowulf*, they created wresting stats complete with wrestling monikers. Grendel became known as "Mama's Boy," and posters with pictures of the fighters and their stats adorned the walls of the classroom. What happened was remarkable. Students were engaged, grades were up, and all seemed to be going well. I still had one question, however. Could this type of non-linear, kinesthetic learning translate into higher scores on standardized tests, which were very linear in structure?

The answer came at the end of the school year when teachers gathered to hear the results of Terra Nova scores delivered. I overheard one of the counselors (who was looking over the English scores) say, "What happened here?" The person she was speaking to pointed at me. I became alarmed and worried that my students' scores had dropped. To my great relief, I soon discovered that their scores had improved tremendously. My students had engaged in hard work, but they had not viewed it as work. They were engaged in the learning process together, and they retained information that translated to the linear, standardized tests that they had to take every year. So what was different between this and my current students' active engagement with technology?

WHAT WE KNOW ABOUT THE LEARNING PROCESS

According to the late Seymour Papert, noted MIT researcher and expert on child development and educational technologies, computers have long demonstrated the potential to grant the individual the power to direct his or her own educational progress. Papert, who studied with globally recognized and revered child psychology expert Jean Piaget, believed that computers would inevitably lead to the demise of the education system as we have known it for over 150 years. Papert's Constructionist Theory of Learning relies on the belief that people build knowledge most effectively when they are actively engaged in constructing things in the world (Papert & Harel, 1991).

During the five years that Papert studied with Piaget, his views of learning were shaped by Piaget's concepts of schemas and cognitive equilibrium. Papert came to believe that true learning can only occur when the learner becomes an active participant in the learning process rather than a passive receiver of information. Constructionist learning relies on the learner's ability to create mental models (what Piaget refers to as schemas) in order to better understand the world around him. This theory sees learning not simply as the transmission of knowledge, but rather as a re-construction of knowledge (Oppenheimer, 2003).

Piaget's theory was developed in 1952, and he took note of children's desires to actively explore the world around them to make sense of it and used this information to develop his four stages of cognitive development. The four stages he identified were as follows: The sensorimotor stage from birth to age two; the preoperational stage from age two to age seven; the concrete operational stage from age seven to age eleven; and the formal operational stage, which begins in adolescence and spans through adulthood.

In the sensorimotor stage, infants and toddlers acquire information through sensory experiences. Object permanence is developed during this stage, and infants and toddlers begin to distinguish between what is permanent and what is transitory. In the preoperational stage, children learn mainly through pretend play. At this point, they begin to develop schemas that will reinforce cognitive equilibrium, which is defined as "when a child's existing schemas are capable of explaining what it can perceive around it, it is said to be in a state of equilibrium, i.e. a state of cognitive balance" (Piaget, 1962, as cited in Burnett, 2010, p. 145). The schemas that children must develop to achieve a state of balance could be likened to building blocks of learning, and children develop these schemas through play by connecting what they know about the world to new ideas and concepts. They use this process to test existing schemas and to create cognitive equilibrium. A temporary barrier to comprehension could occur if an interruption, such as the introduction of a new mode of obtaining information, occurs (Piaget, 1962).

As a child gets older, thinking becomes more logical in the concrete operational stage. During this stage, children may still struggle with abstract concepts. As they learn how to apply logic to these concepts, more complex ideas may be introduced. During this phase of development, children become less egocentric and begin to understand that their thoughts are unique to them and that others may not share their thoughts or feelings. Children begin to comprehend things on a different level at this stage of development. Stories can now be connected to personal experiences, and meaning may be taken from those stories as new schemas are formed. When information is not presented in a logical fashion or is too abstract in nature, it can become a barrier to comprehension as the child struggles to see the connection between what she already knows and what the story is telling her. The ability to predict the outcome of the story is important during this stage of development(Piaget, 1962).

Piaget places adolescence in the formal operational stage. It is at this stage that logic increases, and the individual begins to use deductive reasoning and can understand more abstract concepts. Adolescents begin to problem solve by comparing existing schemas to new schemas that are developed through exposure to new experiences. Multiple potential solutions to problems begin to emerge. It is at this stage that more complex concepts in literary texts should be introduced. A barrier to reading comprehension in this stage could occur for a variety of reasons such as lack of decoding skills resulting in limited fluency for more complex texts or lack of exposure to pertinent vocabulary.

Piaget saw children's intellectual development as a qualitative rather than a quantitative process. He did not just see cognitive development occurring through the addition of information. He believed that children undergo specific changes in how they think as they grow older (Piaget, 1952). This very belief may be exactly what needs to be taken into consideration as we review the disruptive nature of technology in the 21st century. These stages of development must be taken into consideration as we determine not only *where* but also *when* technology should be introduced to enhance educational outcomes. It occurred to me that what had changed was not so much the method and its effectiveness as it was the potential destructive nature of the technology (when introduced too early) on the capacity of the individual to think and process information.

This causes me to reflect, once again, on Systems Thinking. Donatella Meadows (2008), believed that disruption can lead to reorganization, and reorganization can lead to the dawn of a new way of thinking. This is usually the aim of systems thinking. Meadows reminds us that human beings prefer to think in linear patterns because linear relationships are easier to conceptualize. We can draw linear relationships with a straight line, and they appear logical because they produce a proportional effect. Nonlinear relationships, however, may create discomfort. The relationship between the cause and the effect can only be envisioned with a curved or wiggly line connecting the two. The route is not clearly defined. But we must remember that we live in a world filled with nonlinearities, and, as Meadow says, "Nonlinearities are important not only because they confound our expectations about the relationship between action and response. They are even more important because they change the relative strengths of feedback loops. They can flip a system from one mode of behavior to another" (Meadows, 2008, p. 92).

What does this mean as we consider the course of education in the 21st century? Should we continue to engage in the linear processes developed over hundreds of years and trust that they will ensure a prosperous future for generations to come, or should we take into consideration the theories of Piaget, Papert, and Meadows and reenvision education as an active, dynamic process that is capable of, and possibly even in need of, change? The answer may just be that we need to use our integrative-thinking processes to develop a system that is able to capture the best parts of both systems. If this occurs, we could potentially create one of the most beneficial and exciting systems ever known to man.

The next few chapters will present the data obtained from the study that I conducted to determine the effectiveness of both traditional means of literacy instruction and literacy instruction delivered primarily via the iPad. As you read the information provided about when, where, why, and how the data was collected, please keep in mind what you have read thus far. This data is being presented in the hopes that it will begin a discussion about the potential of integrative processes and how we can use these processes to lead to a more engaging and productive system of education for our students.

CHAPTER 9

RESEARCH DESIGN, EFFECT SIZE AND METHODOLOGY

As I began teaching literacy skills by incorporating the multimodalities of the iPad into my lessons, I became interested in knowing if the iPad had demonstrated effectiveness as an educational tool, particularly as it pertained to the instruction of reading. I launched an extensive review of existing research hoping to find information that might help me to more effectively use the iPad in the high school setting. I soon discovered that information regarding the use of the iPad to mitigate literacy deficits was scarce. Because the iPad and its unique combination of applications and multimodal features (those that apply to multiple senses) had not been effectively measured in educational settings, I realized that there was a pronounced gap in the existing literature.

One obvious reason for the lack of credible studies was the fact that the use of the iPad in classrooms across the country was fairly new, and it was limited in scope due to the cost. It simply had not been around long enough nor had it been used in enough settings for longitudinal data to be collected and analyzed. I also knew that as an educator in a special program aimed at improving literacy achievement, I had collected pre- and post-test extant data that covered three years of iPad instruction as well as two years of pre-iPad instruction, and I felt that this data could be used to fill a small part of this gap.

The Rise of the Human Digital Brain:
How Multidirectional Thinking is Changing the Way We Learn, pages 83–93.

THE RESEARCH DESIGN

As an educator who taught within this specialized program designed to target literacy deficits, I collected pre- and post-test data from a norm-referenced reading assessment known as the Nelson-Denny Reading Test (NDRT). This test has two components: comprehension and vocabulary. I wanted to measure growth in both areas. The growth that I sought to measure may have occurred as a result of what I termed as "extended literacy learning opportunities" as well as the use of the iPad for literacy instruction. For the purposes of my study, the term "extended literacy learning opportunities" was defined as "providing multiple means of representation, action, expression, and engagement with adaptations to presentation formats provided during classroom instructional time as well as during additional time (in the case of this study, 50% more time) to introduce these learning opportunities to students" (Bulgren, Graner, & Deschler, 2013, p. 18). Additionally, I used traditional literacy instruction, which for the purposes of my study referred to the use of bound books, worksheets, workbooks, and handouts.

As I prepared to conduct my study, I took the two years of data collected prior to the introduction of the iPad for literacy instruction and the three years of data collected after the iPad had been introduced as a tool for literacy instruction and analyzed it. My goal was to review the data of the 95 participants and to compare growth in both vocabulary and comprehension in the two groups both prior to the introduction of the iPad and after the introduction of the iPad for literacy instruction.

One purpose of the study was to determine if the program demonstrated a statistically significant difference on the attainment of literacy skills (to include vocabulary and comprehension achievement) for students in the reading program over the course of five years. A statistically significant difference is found when a low probability of getting a result that large or larger exists; therefore, when a statistically significant difference occurs, it is statistically improbable that the results may be attributed to chance.

A second purpose was to determine if the introduction of extended literacy learning opportunities without the introduction of the iPad created a statistically significant difference on vocabulary and comprehension achievement. A third and final purpose of the study was to determine if iPad-based literacy instruction had a greater influence on reading achievement scores in vocabulary, comprehension, and overall literacy attainment than the introduction of extended literacy learning opportunities alone. This study was also conducted with the purpose of measuring the effect size of any growth that may have occurred over the course of the freshman year when students were exposed to the independent variables of extended literacy learning opportunities and iPad-based reading instruction.

My research consisted of two phases of extant (existing) data analysis. In the first phase, separate paired-samples *t*-tests (which are used to compare pre- and post-test results) were conducted to compare the means of reading achievement scores in vocabulary, comprehension, and composite scores for all students enrolled in the reading program. Next, separate paired-samples *t*-tests were conducted to compare the means of pre- and post-program reading achievement scores in vocabulary, comprehension, and composite scores from students in the pre-iPad group (from 2010–2012). Finally, separate paired-samples *t*-tests were conducted to compare the means of pre- and post-program reading achievement scores in vocabulary, comprehension, and composite scores from students in the iPad group (2012–2013 and 2014–2016).

The second phase of data analysis consisted of a pre-post gains analysis comparing the pre-iPad and iPad literacy groups' gains in vocabulary, comprehension, and composite scores. Independent-samples *t*-tests (which compare the means of two samples that are independent and not from randomly assigned groups) were conducted to compare the means of the two groups. The gains of the iPad group (treatment group) versus the gains of the non-iPad group (control group) were compared to determine if a statistically significant difference could be identified between the two as well as to determine the effect size of any growth that may have occurred.

EFFECT SIZE

While a statistically significant difference is important when measuring research outcomes, it does not aid in pinpointing the magnitude of the effect of a given treatment. An effect size would need to be determined to do this. According to Robert Coe, author of a paper entitled "It's the Effect Size, Stupid: What Effect Size Is and Why It Is Important," the effect size, or Cohen's *d*, is "a way of quantifying the size of the difference between two groups. Its greatest value can be found when it is used to measure the effectiveness of a particular intervention as it relates to some comparison" (p. 1). The effect size was developed as a way to measure educational outcomes in relation to the impact of various intervention strategies (such as extended time, smaller class size, use of technology, etc.) by comparing outcomes of treated versus non-treated groups. John Hattie, author of the 2008 book *Visible Learning*, sought to determine which interventions had the biggest impact on student success, so he reviewed over 800 meta-analyses of over 50,000 studies and synthesized the information to create average effect sizes for various treatments. This resulted in a list of skills that researchers now focus upon to measure the effects of standard treatments. In this way, researchers and educators are better able to determine what is working in the classroom.

Effect sizes are used to quantify the impact of a particular teaching intervention on student learning. For example, an effect size of 0.20 would be considered a small effect size and would indicate that the intervention did very little to extend learning beyond that which would be typically expected after one school year of exposure. An effect size of 0.40 would be considered the "hinge point," or the point at which a measurable difference could be detected. An effect size of 0.50 would be considered a medium effect size, and this would indicate that the intervention extended learning beyond that which would typically be expected over the course of one school year. An effect size of 0.80 or greater would be considered a large effect size, and this would indicate that the intervention extended learning well beyond what might be expected over the course of a typical school year.

TYPES OF LITERACY INSTRUCTION AND EFFECT SIZES

When students are provided with direct instruction, defined as "the explicit teaching of a skill-set using lectures or demonstrations of the material to students," (Fisher et al., 2016, p. 8), it typically creates an effect size measured at 0.59. This would be considered a medium effect size, and it would stretch beyond that typically attained over the course of one year of school. In his 2012 book *Visible Learning for Teachers*, Hattie noted that students can complete up to 90% of classroom instruction using only surface-level skills. As noted earlier, surface-level reading skills are defined as "strategies that involve initial access to text comprehension such as adjusting reading speed, omitting unknown words, and re-reading" (Cantrell & Carter, 2009, p. 201). Although this type of learning is critical, it does not reinforce deep-level reading skills, which are defined as "strategies that cause readers to engage in the text in a meaningful way, including visualization, note taking, paraphrasing, underlining and discussing reading with others" (Cantrell & Carter, 2009, p. 201). Surface-level skills are often used when teaching students the mechanics of reading, and deep-level reading skills that reinforce vocabulary attainment and comprehension are often over looked during the early stages of literacy education.

Surface-level reading strategies mainly consist of decoding skills, which are necessary to develop successful reading habits. Vocabulary and comprehension, on the other hand, are categorized as deep-level reading strategies because they require more exposure and reinforcement, and they are not static. These strategies reinforce meaning, and they continue to develop as the reader matures and is exposed to greater vocabulary and more difficult pieces of literature. Deep-level reading strategies can have a strong effect on the acquisition of knowledge and the attainment of skill (Fisher et al., 2016).

Vocabulary instruction plays a key role in literacy attainment. A strong vocabulary program would demonstrate an effect size of 0.67 or greater (Fisher et al., 2016). While teaching vocabulary, which (if taught effectively) is itself a deep-level reading strategy, students must be taught for depth and transfer. According to Michael Graves, author of *Vocabulary Learning and Instruction* (1986), vocabulary should be viewed across five dimensions: generalization through definitional knowledge, application through correct usage, breadth through recall of words, precision through understanding examples and non-examples, and availability through use of vocabulary in discussion (as cited in Fisher et al., 2016). Many times, vocabulary acquisition is taught as a surface-level reading strategy, and these five dimensions are not taken into account. In other words, mere exposure to words is not enough to increase the depth and breadth of an individual's vocabulary. The vocabulary skills necessary for success must be taught through repetition, contextualization, and authentic reasons for using the words in class discussions, reading assignments, and writing assignments (Fisher et al., 2016).

The ultimate goal of reading should be comprehension. According to John Hattie (2012), a strong comprehension program would demonstrate an effect size of 0.60 or greater. Reading comprehension is achieved through a variety of instructional methods designed to help students analyze and organize information and then link that information to the world around them, reflect upon it, and act (Fisher et al., 2016). Reading comprehension is a way to acquire depth of knowledge and then to transfer that information to existing schemas, and it should result in integrative reading skills rather than strategic ones. If automaticity, which is defined as "the ability to do things without having to think about them" (Tzelgov, 1999, p. 3), is achieved, students will not be *forced* to make a prediction or to create a visual image; rather, these processes will occur automatically.

Strong reading-comprehension programs may start with the teacher modeling for students how to find the main idea, annotate literature, and develop summaries. Students are then gradually guided to do this themselves. Successful annotation of texts may include underlining, circling, and making margin notes to improve student understanding of new knowledge and build capacity to engage in study skills. The common effect size for reading comprehension programs is 0.63, which equates to a medium effect size (Fisher et al., 2016). Teaching these skills in isolation will not deliver the desired results, so direct modeling while reading an assigned text would be a desired method of instruction for teaching appropriate study skills.

Students will also need time to consolidate new learning. While educators often assume that new information is more easily recalled directly after instruction, this is not necessarily the case. Recall is usually better 24 hours after exposure to new information (Henderson, Weighall, & Gaskell, 2013). Students should be given time to return to new learning again and again over time in order to further enhance and ingrain information successfully. Rehearsal, memorization, and feedback are important steps in consolidating new information (Fisher et al., 2016). These are surface-level strategies that should lead to deeper-level learning as students begin to interact with content and ideas and to link those new concepts to existing knowledge.

Fluency in reading increases as students move from surface-level to deep-level reading strategies (Topping, 2006). Repeated reading is one way that an adolescent who has not gained sufficient fluency can be assisted. Repeated reading is a method of instruction in which a student listens to a passage as it is read by a teacher and then reads the same passage to himself before finally reading it aloud. Rate, accuracy, and prosody are calculated and reported to the students with the goal being an increase in all three with subsequent attempts (Fisher et al., 2016).

Effect size for computer-assisted instruction. The average effect size for computer assisted instruction is 0.37, which equates to a small effect size (Fisher et al, 2016). According to Hattie (2009), although this equates to a small effect size, it would still be equivalent to what would extend beyond that attained over the course of one year of education due to its proximity to the hinge point of 0.40. *Visible Learning for Teachers: Maximizing Impact on Learning* (2012) refers to computer-assisted instruction as the availability of access to the internet and the use of word processing functions.

Effect size for response to intervention. The effect size for response to intervention (RTI) is 1.07, which equates to a large effect size and would represent potentially two- to three-years of growth beyond that attained over the course of a typical school year (Fisher et al., 2016). RTI interventions are broken down into three tiers. In an academic system, the first tier includes universal screening for all students, and all students receive treatment. The second tier includes a more targeted group that may lack some of the necessary skills for success. This group would receive more time and intensity of instruction. The third tier includes students who lag significantly behind their peers (one year or more) and who demonstrate weak progress on screening measures (Fisher et al., 2016). Tier-three groups require more intensive interventions. Programs aimed at mitigating vocabulary and comprehension skill deficits of low-achieving students would potentially find stronger outcomes by instituting an RTI program. The participants in my study would be considered a tier-three group.

Intensive intervention is defined as "a process involving adaptation of secondary interventions (Tier 2) that are more frequently and concretely quantitative rather than qualitative adaptations to interventions" (National Center on Intensive Intervention, 2013, p. 31). These types of interventions would include implementing a system of data collection and progress monitoring that includes determining both level and growth rate. The use of repeated reading instruction would also be considered an intensive intervention strategy. Creating small groups for instruction and individualizing instruction and assessment would also be considered intensive interventions. Small group learning has an effect size of 0.49, and this would equate to a medium effect size indicative of growth beyond that expected over the course of one school year (Fisher et al., 2016).

Effect size for repeated reading programs. The average effect size for repeated reading programs is 0.67, which equates to a medium effect size. Because this effect size is greater than the hinge point of 0.40, it would equate to an effect size that would stretch beyond that typically attained over the course of one year of school (Fisher et al., 2016). According to Melanie Kuhn and Steven Stahl (2003), authors of a study on reading automaticity, repeated reading programs have been shown to improve reading rate outcomes because students practice reading over the same text multiple times and are presented with models of fluency through audio tapes or adult oral readings prior to practicing themselves. Although repeated reading programs have been shown to improve fluency, they do not necessarily improve accuracy or comprehension. To more greatly affect

TABLE 9.1. Effect Size: Types of Instruction

Type of Instruction	Cohen's d
Direct Instruction	0.59
Vocabulary Instruction	0.67
Comprehension Instruction	0.60
Computer Assisted Instruction	0.37
Response to Intervention	1.07
Repeated Reading	0.67

Source: Fisher, Frey and Hattie, 2016, Appendix, Effect Size

comprehension and accuracy, students must be able to apply these improvements to unpracticed passages (as cited in Wexler et al., 2010). The effect sizes for the various elements of literacy instruction commonly present in literacy programs are listed in Table 9.1.

METHODOLOGY

This study used a quasi-experimental non-equivalent control group design since the comparison groups (pre-iPad and post-iPad groups) were not randomized, contained a pre-treatment and post-treatment measure, had a treated and untreated group, and the groups were measured using an analysis of covariance using post-test minus pre-test measure to evaluate the effect of the treatment being introduced.

Participants in the study were 95 (N=95) freshman, adolescent male reading students at a large Mid-Western high school. Thirty-seven (n=37) of the participants received no iPad instruction and all methods of literacy instruction were traditional and involved no technology other than the use of electronic slide presentations and word processing platforms. Fifty-eight (n=58) of the participants in the iPad group received literacy instruction both through the iPad and through extended literacy learning opportunities, and traditional literacy instruction.

DEPENDENT AND INDEPENDENT VARIABLES

The independent variables in the study were the extended literacy learning opportunities designed to mitigate literacy deficits in part one of the study, and the introduction of iPad-based reading instruction in part two of the study. The dependent variables were the pre- and post-test comprehension, vocabulary, and composite scores on the Nelson-Denny Reading Test (NDRT). In part one of the study, pre- and post-assessment pairs of test scores served as the dependent variable for examination, while part two of the study employed gains in achievement between pre- and post-NDRT administrations as a single dependent variable.

INSTRUMENTATION

The Nelson-Denny Reading Test (NDRT) is a widely-used assessment of vocabulary and reading comprehension that is comprised of two subtests, vocabulary and comprehension. The vocabulary section consists of 80 multiple choice items, and the comprehension section contains seven reading passages and a total of 38 questions. NDRT raw scores in reading comprehension and vocabulary were tabulated and converted to scale scores using the Raw Score to Scale Score Conversions Extended-Time Administration Table. The comprehension scale scores were multiplied by two and added to the vocabulary scale scores to arrive at a composite scale score (V + 2C), and composite scale scores were compared for statistical significance.

According to James Brown, Vivian Fishco, and Gerald Hanna, authors of the NDRT Manual for Scoring and Interpretation (1993), NDRT scale scores are recommended for assessing growth over a period of time. These scores possess the equal-interval characteristic that is important for certain statistical-calculations. Scale scores range from 125 to 258 and are "based upon the pooled standardization samples from grades 10, 11, and 12, both two-year college classes, and both lower-division classes in the four-year institutions. The unweighted pooled distribution from these seven reference groups has been converted into a system of normalized scale score for which the mean is set at 200 and the standard deviation at 25" (p. 14).

MODES OF INSTRUCTION

Modes of instruction varied between the control group (Group 1, 2010–2011 and 2011–2012) and the treatment group (Group 2, 2012–2013 and 2014–2015, and 2015–2016 combined). Group 1 consisted of 37 (n=37) students who received traditional reading instruction, which included the use of class novel sets, library research, and the use of novels of choice. A variety of short stories (found in anthologies) were also used. The anthologies chosen were *Retold Classics,* and the stories contained within these anthologies are rewritten at lower Lexile levels (while still maintaining the details of the original stories) to promote greater comprehension for students demonstrating reading skills that fall one year or more below grade level.

A Lexile measure for reading is "an approach to reading and text measurement. There are two Lexile measures: the Lexile reader measure, and the Lexile text measure. A Lexile reader measure represents a person's reading ability on the Lexile scale. A Lexile text measure represents a text's level on the Lexile scale" (MetaMetrics, 2009). Reader measures were determined using the Nelson-Denny grade-equivalent scores and Lexile text measures were considered when selecting appropriate literary pieces for instruction. Current events articles taken from magazines and newspapers were also used, but Lexile levels were not changed in these samples.

The use of novel-of-choice reading was an important component of this program. Penny Kittle, author of the 2013 book *Book Love: Developing Depth, Stamina, and Passion in Adolescent Readers,* believes that boys' literacy skills will increase when they are given an opportunity to choose what they read. A major component of this program was access to appropriate and interesting reading material. This was achieved by (as noted earlier in this book) working closely with the school librarian to select a wide array of novels that traditionally appeal to male readers. These novels were also selected for readability, and by the end of an extensive search, a library consisting of more than 250 possible selections for low-achieving male adolescent readers was achieved.

Additionally, I reviewed sites such as guysread.com and attended conferences aimed at introducing male-friendly literature to high school libraries, and I made interesting new book selections for the school's library based on this research. Novels were selected not only for readability but also for interest level. Once the selections were acquired, an electronic presentation including both pictures and summaries of all the books selected for inclusion in the program was created and made available to the students through a school-wide platform. Book talks were also implemented to encourage students to find books that would fit individual interests, thus encouraging deeper reading to take place.

Vocabulary instruction included the use of visual modes of instruction through electronic presentations delivered during class instruction. These presentations included visual representations of words through pictures as well as instruction on the use of context clues to create and derive meaning. The only form of technology used by Group 1 was a class set of computers for word processing or for creating electronic presentations. Both groups 1 and 2 were presented with interactive electronic presentations that started with an example of an assigned vocabulary word used in context. Students were then invited to use the context clues to create a definition for the word. Next, the students were provided the definition and a picture, via the electronic presentation, to associate with the word. The electronic presentation was made available to the students for study purposes via a school-wide platform. Students were also repeatedly exposed to new and old vocabulary to ensure that vocabulary attainment was reinforced. Once a vocabulary list was exhausted, the words on that list continued to be reinforced throughout the school year using a variety of means, to include assessments. Students were also required to identify five new vocabulary words per week from class reading (either novel of choice reading or other pieces introduced throughout the course of the week). These words would be included on subsequent assessments for individual students. The words also had to be used in sentences with strong context clues, and pictures associated with the words were required as well.

Group 2 consisted of 58 (n=58) students who received some forms of traditional instruction coupled with reading instruction delivered via the iPad. This group also received traditional instruction using anthologies such as *Retold Classics* and novels of choice. In this case, the novels of choice could be downloaded onto the iPad in the form of iBooks for students to take advantage of the multimodalities of the iPad for instruction such as the text-to-voice feature. Students were also provided direct instruction on how to create reading notes and how to effectively use the highlighting feature available via iBooks. Students were also taught during direct instruction how to search for information in iBooks and how to organize notes. Students were then allowed to use their texts and notes for reading quizzes, so the addition of notes and highlighting had an impact on student success. This teaching method was designed to reinforce deep-reading skills that would lead to greater comprehension.

For vocabulary instruction, students downloaded and created vocabulary lists containing visual images and flash cards using an online Quizlet application and using Keynote, an electronic media presentation application. Students used the voice-to-text feature of the iPad's word processing application Pages to create vocabulary sentences and reading summaries. Students participated in group work as they shared and revised work, and they created book talks accompanied by iPad images to represent various literary terms as they found them in the stories. Students read current events articles via Newsela, an interactive website that allows students to determine appropriate Lexile levels for reading and then to take quizzes to measure comprehension. Approximately 70% of reading and vocabulary instruction was delivered via the iPad by 2014.

Both groups were provided with extended literacy learning opportunities. These opportunities included smaller class size (under 15), frequent small group work opportunities, repeated reading instruction, and an additional one-half year of reading instruction. Both groups were also provided with multiple means of representation, action and expression, and engagement with adaptations to presentation formats provided during classroom instructional time.

DATA COLLECTION

The data were all collected using the same methods. An initial NDRT reading assessment was given prior to a student's participation in a year-long reading program. The reading program consisted of seven to eight 45-minute blocks of literacy instruction per week. A second NDRT reading assessment was given at the end of the school year. The data from both tests were collected and used to record summary data from both the pre- and post-tests. Scale scores from pre- and post-test administration were used for subsequent analysis.

In part one of the study, I collected pre- and post-test vocabulary and comprehension scores and created an overall composite score for both administrations by adding the NDRT vocabulary scores to NDRT reading scores, which were multiplied by 2 to create a single dependent variable. I then conducted separate paired-samples *t*-tests comparing vocabulary, comprehension, and composite results to evaluate the: (1) overall effect of pre- and post-program scores in the reading program for all years studied, (2) pre-iPad instruction, and (3) iPad-based instruction.

In the second part of the study, I separated the participants into two groups: pre-iPad and iPad-based instruction. Dummy coding was used to identify the groups with "1" being pre-iPad and "2" being iPad-based instruction. A composite gain score was developed by subtracting the composite score at the end of the program from the composite score at the beginning. I then used an Independent Samples *t*-test to examine differences between the pre-iPad and iPad-based instruction groups for vocabulary, comprehension, and composite results.

Once the results, which will be shared in the next chapter, were available, I was both happy with yet puzzled by them. It appeared that my students were making tremendous gains in both vocabulary and comprehension skills; however, the iPad was not yielding the type of results that I had expected.

CHAPTER 10

THE IMPACT OF iPAD MULTIMODALITIES ON THE LITERACY SKILLS OF ADOLESCENT MALES IDENTIFIED AS LOW-ACHIEVING READERS

THE RESULTS

As I analyzed the results of the study, the first thing that I looked for was a statistically significant difference in both the iPad and the pre-iPad groups in vocabulary and comprehension skills. The vocabulary scores for the pre-iPad population demonstrated a significant increase from pre-test to post-test ($t(36) = 4.27$, $p < .05$). This indicates that a statistically significant difference was yielded in vocabulary achievement when students were involved in extended literacy learning opportunities. The use of visuals, multiple means of expression, context clues, and the creation of vocabulary tests that were not at the lowest level of Bloom's

The Rise of the Human Digital Brain:
How Multidirectional Thinking is Changing the Way We Learn, pages 95–99.

Taxonomy had yielded statistically significant gains in vocabulary attainment for my students.

The comprehension scores for the pre-iPad population also demonstrated a significant increase from pre-test to post-test ($t(36) = 6.82, p <. 05$). This indicates that a statistically significant difference was achieved using extended literacy learning opportunities that included close reading, rereading, reading of choice, use of plot pyramids, and frequent class discussion and presentation of what was read. Quizzes and tests also moved to the higher level of Bloom's Taxonomy to focus on synthesis an analysis rather than simple knowledge of what was read.

Next was an analysis of the iPad group's scores. Vocabulary scores for the group that used both extended literacy learning opportunities as well as the iPad for vocabulary instruction also showed a statistically significant level of growth ($t(57) = 4.15, p < .05$). The same was true for comprehension scores in the iPad group, which also demonstrated a statistically significant level of growth ($t(57) = 5.08, p < .05$).

I was pleased to see that both the pre-iPad and iPad groups had demonstrated statistically significant growth, but to truly understand the impact of these interventions, I needed to compare the effect sizes of both groups.

CALCULATING EFFECT SIZE FOR THE STUDY

In the realm of using effect size with educational research, Douglas Fisher, Nancy Frey, and John Hattie (2016), determined that an effect size of 1.0 is typically associated with improving student achievement by 84% in groups receiving a specific treatment as compared to groups who did not receive similar treatments and is equivalent to a two to three-year leap in performance, while an effect size of 0.50 is equivalent to a one grade leap (Table 10.1). An effect size above 0.40 is above average for educational research, and according to Hattie (2012), when actions are in the 0.40 and above range, data suggests that learning extends beyond that which would be expected from attending school for one year.

For the results of this study to show a significant impact on learning, I was hoping for results at 0.50 or above. That would indicate that growth would be more than what would be expected from one year of education. I was very pleased to find that in all instances, my students growth exceeded expectations. In vo-

TABLE 10.1. Effect Size Interpretation

Cohen's d	Interpretation of Effect Size
0.20	Small effect size
0.50	Medium effect size
0.80	Large effect size

Source: Fisher, Frey and Hattie, 2016, Appendix, Effect Size

TABLE 10.2. Effect Size Estimates for Literacy Program Elements

	Pre-iPad	iPad	Combined
Vocabulary	0.70	0.54	0.59
Comprehension	1.18	0.66	0.83
Combined (V + 2C)	1.26	0.91	1.03

cabulary, both groups had Cohen's *d* scores that exceeded 0.50, and the growth in comprehension in both groups also had Cohen's *d* scores that exceed 0.50, thus indicating that growth was greater than what would be expected from one year of instruction in a traditional school setting.

Table 10.2. demonstrates the effect sizes of both groups in vocabulary and comprehension as well as the combined scores of both. As the data above illustrates, both the pre-iPad and iPad groups had a medium effect size in vocabulary, but the pre-iPad group out-performed the iPad group by 0.16. In comprehension the difference in the results are much more pronounced. We know that an effect size of 1.0 is typically associated with improving student achievement by 84% in groups receiving a specific treatment as compared to groups who did not receive similar treatments and is equivalent to a two to three-year leap in performance. The pre-iPad group actually performed better than 1.0 with a Cohen's *d* of 1.18. This showed that a great deal of success was achieved in reading comprehension when traditional methods of literacy instruction were used.

The iPad group also had better than average results. With an effect size of 0.66, the students did better than would be expected over the course of a typical school year, and this score also exceeded Hattie's average effect size for a comprehension program, which was set at .60. However, the difference between the two scores leads to some serious questions regarding why the addition of the iPad caused a decrease in gains from previous years.

FINDINGS

Analysis of the data revealed that when extended literacy learning opportunities were employed to increase comprehension and vocabulary achievement, a statistically significant impact on achievement was demonstrated. Both the pre-iPad and the iPad groups demonstrated statistically significant growth in vocabulary with a medium effect size. In comprehension, both the pre-iPad and iPad groups demonstrated statistically significant growth with a large effect size. The largest effect size was achieved in both groups when extended literacy learning opportunities were provided. As a whole, the reading program studied achieved a large effect size in vocabulary and comprehension (1.03) and impacted literacy skills by adding two to three years of growth over the course of one school year.

Vocabulary results. Both the use of extended literacy learning opportunities and the use of the iPad for vocabulary instruction yielded statistically significant growth. While both the pre-iPad and the iPad groups showed significant growth, the use of the iPad for vocabulary instruction did not yield a greater improvement of vocabulary results over pre-iPad vocabulary results. In fact, there was no statistically significant difference between vocabulary achievement before the introduction of the iPad and after its introduction.

Both the pre-iPad and iPad groups demonstrated medium effect sizes for vocabulary with the combined effect size for vocabulary of both groups being 0.59. This indicates that more gains in vocabulary achievement were attained than would typically be expected over the course of one school year. The pre-iPad group demonstrated an effect size of 0.70, which exceeds Hattie's average effect size of 0.67 for vocabulary programs. The iPad group's effect size of 0.54 fell below Hattie's average effect size for vocabulary programs but still indicated growth beyond that expected over the course of a typical school year.

Comprehension results. In comprehension, both the pre-iPad and the iPad groups demonstrated statistically significant growth. However, there was a statistically significant difference between the achievement scores of the two groups. The pre-iPad group demonstrated a large effect size of 1.18, indicating that those in the treated group demonstrated two to three years of growth over the course of one school year. The iPad group demonstrated a medium effect size of 0.66, indicating that more than one year of growth occurred over the course of one school year. The combined effect size for both groups was 0.83, which equates to a large effect size overall and demonstrates that the program impacted comprehension at a much greater rate than would typically be expected.

Extended literacy learning opportunities. This study shows that there is a positive relationship between extended literacy learning opportunities and comprehension and vocabulary achievement. There is also a positive relationship between multimodal opportunities via the iPad coupled with extended literacy learning opportunities for comprehension and vocabulary achievement, but to a lesser degree than extended literacy learning opportunities coupled with traditional literacy instruction. While the findings between the two groups show a positive relationship between the treatments and the outcomes, they also demonstrate that there is a larger impact on comprehension when the treatment of extended literacy learning opportunities is applied without the addition of the iPad.

iPad multimodalities. The results of this study support the potential benefits of iPad multimodalities and their impact on reading outcomes for low-achieving adolescent male readers. The use of the iPad for comprehension and vocabulary instruction yielded statistically significant results, and medium effect sizes were produced in both comprehension and vocabulary. The results of this study indicate that while the use of iPad multimodalities may yield a statistically significant difference in comprehension and vocabulary outcomes, this impact was not as large as outcomes created by extended literacy learning opportunities introduced without the use of the iPad.

Technology and comprehension. The results of this study could also be interpreted to mean that the linear thought processes reinforced for hundreds of years through rote practice are now changing to multidirectional, nonlinear patterns. This is happening due to the ubiquitous nature of 21st century technology and its reinforcement of more multidirectional patterns of thought (Wolf & Barzillai, 2009). The students in group 1 (pre-iPad group) of this study were not exposed to the same type of technology (such as the iPad) at as early an age as the students in group 2 (iPad group). The technology simply did not exist in the same form when the pre-iPad group was in grade school (Davidson, 2011; Kaku, 2014).

ANALYSIS OF RESULTS

As I reviewed the results of the data and applied what I knew about the variables and what I had seen in the way of changes in my students, I reached some startling conclusions. Based on these results, could I definitively say that my current students were not as knowledgeable as previous groups of students? I did not think this was a logical conclusion. Could I say that previous groups were better at analysis of data? I began to understand that while students in 2015 had direct access to much more information (as a result of continuous access to technology) than students in 2010 did, they also had a limited understanding of how to effectively analyze and synthesize this information. If the strengths of the 2010 student were coupled with the strengths of the 2015 student, what might the outcome be? This is a question that has yet to be answered, but it is one that certainly needs to be explored.

CHAPTER 11

HEEDING THE CALL FOR MORE RESEARCH

As noted in earlier chapters, in 1997 the Director of the National Institute of Child Health and Human Development, in consultation with the Secretary of Education, was given the congressional charge of convene a national panel to conduct a meta-analysis of existing research regarding effective reading instruction in schools. This panel, referred to as the National Reading Panel, was comprised of 14 individuals, and it included leading scientists in reading research, representatives of colleges of education, reading teachers, educational administrators, and parents. The report, published in 2000, was entitled *Teaching Children to Read: An Evidence-Based Assessment of Scientific Research Literature on Reading and Its Implications for Reading.*

This report was the most extensive report on reading outcomes that has been conducted in the United States to date. The panel identified topics requiring more study. Those topics included: optimal length of programs and optimal years; teachers' depth of phonics knowledge; use of scripted programs vs. assessment of individual needs; flexible instruction groups and phonics programs; teacher and student motivational factors; phonics program ingredients that yield best results; contribution of decodable books to phonics effectiveness; effectiveness of phonics beyond 2nd grade; best phonics methods for poor readers above 1st grade; phonics instruction and addressing needs of older students with bad reading habits; and

The Rise of the Human Digital Brain: How Multidirectional Thinking is Changing the Way We Learn, pages 101–109.

systematic instruction in fluency and automaticity for older students' phonics instruction.

The results of my study support the fact that the last two topics identified by the 2000 report are in need of additional research: phonics instruction and addressing needs of older students with bad reading habits, and systematic instruction in fluency and automaticity for older students' phonics instruction (particularly as they apply to male adolescent readers identified as low-achieving readers). Since the report was finalized in the year 2000, technology has advanced to such an extent that its impact on reading instruction should be studied and best practices should be established once more studies have been conducted.

ADOLESCENT MALES AND LITERACY ATTAINMENT

As noted in earlier chapters, one term that emerged from the 2000 reading report was "low-achieving readers." Low-achieving readers are defined as "older children with poor reading progress, varying in intelligence, at least some of whom achieved poorly in other academic areas" (National Reading Panel, 2000, p. 90).

The most recent research on the struggles that boys face in school indicates the need for the identification of methods to reverse some troubling trends that have emerged. Dr. Michael Gurian (2017) notes that "boys receive two-thirds of the Ds and Fs in our schools but less than 40 percent of the As. Overall, there is no racial or ethnic group in which boys are, in overall markers, doing better than girls" (p. 7). Gurian goes on to reveal that there is a 10-point gap between males and females in literacy and that boys are, on average, 1½ years behind girls in literacy skills.

There are a variety of reasons for this, but as the 2000 reading report highlights, the surface-level reading skills of decoding and fluency can be impacted by lack of phonemic awareness. This is particularly true for boys, who tend to learn best via synthetic phonics rather than analytic phonics. Because boys tend to rely more heavily on sounds than on site words when learning to read, any hearing impairment (ear infection, CAPD, etc.) can lead to a delay in decoding skills and thus interfere with reading development (Updike & Thornburg, 1992). This in turn may lead to a lack of fluency, and this can impact a boy's ability to develop surface-level reading skills during the developmentally crucial periods between kindergarten and third grade when the reading brain really develops the most. If the surface-level skills are not fully developed, this may lead to a delay in the development of the deep-level reading skills of comprehension and vocabulary.

TECHNOLOGY AND ADOLESCENT MALE LITERACY INSTRUCTION

Most boys can more effectively activate both sides of the brain when learning new concepts when motion is incorporated into the learning. Because of their natural kinesthetic nature, boys do best when they can touch, feel, and interact with the material they are learning (Reichert & Hawley, 2014). This is one reason why Multimodality Theory should be explored further and implemented in classrooms, particularly since technology has become so ubiquitous in today's society. Multimodality theory "looks at the many different modes that people use to communicate with each other and to express themselves. This theory is relevant as an increase in technology tools, and associated access to multimedia composing software, has led to people being able to easily use many modes in art, writing, music, and dance and every day interactions with each other" (Kresse, 2009, p. 38). To best address the needs of male students, the multimodalities available via the iPad and other forms of technology should be incorporated into classroom teaching when possible and when determined to be an effective means of delivery of information.

In a 2009 study published in *Contemporary Perspectives on Reading and Spelling,* the researchers found that substantial gender differences consistently emerge in the areas of reading attitudes and motivation (as cited in Logan & Johnston, 2010). This study suggested that boys' attitudes or motivations play a more significant role in performance assessments. Differences are also found in self-reported reading frequency, with girls reporting that they read more often than boys.

Associations between reading frequency and comprehension could contribute to differences in reading comprehension performance; however, the same report also indicates that motivation is possibly a larger factor than frequency for boys (Coles & Hall, 2002). This study also found that motivation explained significant variance in reading comprehension performance and that reading frequency did not. Rather, they found that frequent reading with increasingly difficult texts is necessary to impact reading comprehension skills for boys. Background knowledge and vocabulary also have a strong impact on comprehension skills for adolescents, and they have been demonstrated to have the strongest influence on comprehension for 14-year old adolescents; fluency and inference also have large influences on student performance (Lenhard, 2013). If a student has failed to achieve fluency by the time the student enters high school, it will be much more difficult for that student to demonstrate adequate comprehension skills.

In a 2006 article published in *Research in Learning Technology,* Geraldine Price indicated that traditional special education programs encourage the development of metacognition through scaffolding. Assistive technology could be viewed as a technological scaffold. Therefore, the new technology available to 21st century learners can help to assist students who struggle with fluency by creating a scaffold of learning supports that will remove or lessen some of the difficulties involved in the process of reading.

CALL FOR MORE CURRENT RESEARCH

Due to the rapid advances in technology since the last comprehensive reading report was compiled in 2000, it is essential that all current research be explored and that this research be compiled into a new report that can be disseminated to school systems across the country. The rapidly changing nature of technology has created an environment where it is difficult to find research that is current enough to be valid. As I researched for my dissertation, I struggled to find any studies related to literacy, adolescent males, and the use of the iPad to mitigate literacy deficits for this group.

One step in furthering the mission of understanding the impact of digital literacy on educational outcomes would be for the U.S. Department of Education to consider funding new research, particularly regarding the use of multimodalities available via technology to mitigate literacy deficits. It is important that a new meta-analysis of currently existing research be compiled and used to inform instruction. This is indeed the most transformational era in education since the Industrial Age, and we must move quickly to gather and disseminate information that may be used to better inform teaching practices across the country.

MODE OF DELIVERY VERSUS MEANS OF ASSESSMENT

The results of this study may also be interpreted to mean that the disparity in the scores between the pre-iPad and iPad groups is the result of a variance in mode of instruction and means of assessment. The means of assessment for group 1 (pre-iPad group) matched the mode of instruction as both were primarily pencil and paper and very linear in nature. The means of assessment for group 2 (iPad group) continued to be a paper and pencil test, and this did not entirely match the means of instruction, which was primarily iPad based. Existing learning paradigms may be at fault for this discrepancy. According to Bilal Duman (2010), learning occurs through experience, and different learning objectives must be met using a variety of means. Changes in the mode of instruction create changes in brain structure as patterns of thought and existing schemas are challenged (Davidson, 2011; Duman, 2010: Gardner & Davis, 2013; Kaku, 2014). Once new patterns are created and reinforced, assessing them using a different mode could provide inconsistent results.

Cathy Davidson (2011) noted that current linear forms of assessment employed in most school systems may not provide a true picture of what students actually know. In many classrooms today, multidirectional modes of instruction are being employed. These multidirectional modes of instruction often do not match the linear means of assessment. Because the mode of instruction and means of assessment often do not match, the assessments may not be good indicators of whether students are being adequately prepared for the future. A good example of this is the teaching and assessment of vocabulary and comprehension skills. While concepts can easily be taught in classrooms today via the iPad, it is more difficult to measure skills of comprehension and vocabulary attainment using the same mode. This may result in inconsistent outcomes because when the assessment does not match the mode of instruction, the results may be questionable (Gardner & Davis, 2013).

According to Tony Wagner, author of *The Global Achievement Gap* (2014), student creativity may be inhibited when students are exposed to a learning paradigm that focuses more on rote memorization. The iPad does allow for more creativity and may not necessarily reinforce the rote memorization that would support success on a test such as the NDRT. The results of this study could lead to the conclusion that if students had been evaluated in a fashion more consistent with the type of instruction received on the iPad, vocabulary and comprehension outcomes may have been higher.

STRATEGIES FOR VOCABULARY INSTRUCTION

Existing literature regarding vocabulary attainment and comprehension skills also support the findings of this study because the explicit instruction of word attack skills has been shown to have an impact on vocabulary attainment as well as comprehension abilities (Logan & Johnston, 2010). This is particularly true of adolescents who, when asked to read more complex texts, need a greater vocabulary and understanding of syntax; therefore, explicit instruction of vocabulary skills, to include elements of visualization and use of context clues to determine meaning, offer greater opportunities to expand knowledge of vocabulary and to impact overall comprehension (Lenhard, 2013; Nelson et al., 2014; Wolf & Barzillai, 2009). The iPad was used to provide greater opportunities for visualization and to demonstrate the use of vocabulary through multiple means of expression, thus supporting vocabulary acquisition in a new way.

Studies show that by moving students from surface-level reading strategies for literacy attainment to more deep-level reading strategies, comprehension occurs at a higher than average rate (Fisher et al., 2016; Cantrell & Carter, 2009). Surface-level reading strategies include note taking, lecture, and rote memorization. Deep-level reading strategies include multiple interactions with vocabulary in different contexts and activating prior knowledge before and during reading. These strategies can be reinforced in a more hybrid environment that includes both iPad instruction and other modes of instruction.

Similar studies regarding universal design also support the data in this study. *Universal design* a term that refers to "the principles of planning instruction by providing multiple means of representation, providing multiple means of expression and action, and providing multiple means of engagement" (McMahon, 2014, p. 39). In this study, the use of multiple modes of instruction coupled with extended time and smaller class size did have an impact on student comprehension and vocabulary attainment. The use of the iPad for more visual, kinesthetic, and auditory modes of learning was intended to enhance student achievement. The results of this study support this, but they also show that the introduction of the iPad, while still demonstrating a statistically significant growth, did not yield a greater improvement of vocabulary attainment and actually demonstrated a slightly smaller improvement in comprehension than in the pre-iPad group.

BARRIERS TO COMPREHENSION

Children tend to learn through a layered process by first taking in new information and then adapting and applying that new knowledge to previously existing schemas. To achieve cognitive equilibrium, they must first learn how to effectively balance what they know with what they are learning (Piaget, 1952). Twenty-first century students, who are inundated with information that is literally at their fingertips, may find it difficult to distinguish between what is credible information from what is false information. This may result in difficulty achieving the type of balance necessary for true learning to take place. This could lead to 21st century students becoming increasingly susceptible to the power of suggestion. This could also inhibit a student's ability to apply the deep-level learning strategies necessary to achieve cognitive equilibrium.

Additionally, the results of this study may indicate that students may not be receiving enough instruction to reinforce digital literacy requirements. The current Common Core in the United States only has one of the ten anchor standards that pertains to digital or internet literacy. One necessary element of digital literacy that may be taken for granted by educators is the ability to read for meaning on mobile devices. Students who are not taught explicitly how to approach digital texts in a way that supports greater comprehension are more apt to skim over and scan material, thus missing important elements (Larson, 2012; Wolf, 2010).

DISTRACTING FEATURES OF THE IPAD

While the iPad program that the students in this study were exposed to attempted to limit access to games or certain potentially distracting functions (such as instant messaging or alerts), it still could not entirely prevent access. Students who were motivated to use the technology for non-school related use were often able to find ways to do so, and this may have impacted student success. Due to their need to be constantly connected, the availability of games, alerts, and messaging proved to be a distraction for many, particularly for those who had been diagnosed with ADHD. This led to instances where a student would be engaged in reading an iBook and a message would pop up on the screen. This momentary distraction interrupted the flow of information and could potentially have lessened the ability to process and retain information. This could be interpreted to mean that strategies and rules currently in place do not go far enough to encourage proper digital citizenship. Existing strategies also do not go far enough to assure that all the potentials of the iPad as a tool for learning are being realized.

SUPPORTING RESEARCH

The results of this study indicate that extended literacy learning opportunities alone create a larger effect on comprehension than iPad instruction coupled with extended literacy learning opportunities. These findings can also be supported by a 2013 study by Wolfgang Lenhard who compared direct reading strategy instruction with computer-based guided instruction. In this study, nine 6th grade classes of 148 students were followed over the course of one school year and broken into groups equal in number. One group received teacher-directed instructions and the other used a computer-based program called conText. The results of pre- and post-test analysis indicated no differences in comprehension between the two groups. While the results do not indicate that teacher-directed instruction provided a better outcome, they do reinforce the findings that computer-aided literacy instruction does not exceed teacher-directed literacy instruction in comprehension achievement growth.

The National Center for Education Evaluation and Regional Assistance (NCEE) released a report in 2008 entitled *The Enhanced Reading Opportunities Study* that also supports the results of the data in this study. The 2008 report focused on two cohorts of ninth-grade students, each of which was provided with supplemental literacy programs aimed at improving student reading comprehension scores. On average, across the 34 participating high schools, students improved in reading comprehension by 0.08 standard deviations. This represents a statistically significant improvement in students' reading comprehension (p-value =0.042). The addition of extra time and targeted reading instruction used in this program yielded statistically significant growth.

Although the use of extended time and targeted reading instruction were used to enhance learning, both cohorts in the study were treated using two different literacy programs. While the specific use of these programs did yield a statistically significant difference by increasing comprehension by a standard deviation of 0.08, the present study yields larger growth in both comprehension and vocabulary. Both studies indicate that targeted literacy interventions can positively increase comprehension and vocabulary attainment.

TWENTY-FIRST CENTURY EDUCATORS

Another possible interpretation of the results of this study is that the constantly changing nature of technology makes outcomes difficult to measure. With new updates and apps constantly being added, educators are not provided enough time to evaluate the effectiveness of instructional supports. It is difficult to evaluate the effectiveness of one support when it may be abandoned as soon as a "better" one comes along and the first is quickly abandoned. New updates and apps make it difficult for instructors to provide consistency in instructional methods. The novelty of some of the apps and programs can lead educators to attempt to use new methods without having time to fully evaluate the overall effectiveness of those methods.

Many educators are also novices when it comes to use of technology in the classroom, and this learning curve for educators may impact quality of instruction. Additionally, the linear mode of instruction that was practiced in every classroom prior to the introduction of technology as a learning tool is still being practiced, but it is not always the primary mode of instruction in 21st century classrooms.

Students may have different expectations in each class for ways to gather information, and the skill and practice necessary to reinforce learning is not occurring in the same way that it previously did.

Research supports the fact that there is teacher frustration with the ever-changing nature of technology and that there is a need for more professional development. Lotta Larson (2012) conducted a study of pre-service teachers who were invited to participate in an eBook reading experience. All the teachers involved in the study used tablet-based reading devices. The study, which was conducted in 2010, found that only one-fourth of the teachers in the study had read an eBook prior to that point. The teachers did like the opportunities for visualization but noted that there was a predisposition to skim and scan for information, and they felt that the additional features could be distracting.

INTERPRETATION OF FINDINGS REGARDING IPAD MULTIMODALITIES FOR LITERACY INSTRUCTION

These results should not be used to suggest that the iPad is ineffective as a means of literacy instruction. The results support the fact that the use of iPad multimodalities, used in conjunction with other treatments such as extended time and smaller class size, can indeed have a significant impact on comprehension and vocabulary skills. What should be noted is that prior to the introduction of the iPad for classroom instruction, growth was occurring at a larger rate in comprehension and at a similar rate in vocabulary, both deep-level reading skills. The reasons for this should not be strictly attributed to the iPad's introduction to the classroom setting as there were multiple other factors involved. One factor was the neurological changes that may have occurred in the population of students resulting from the ubiquitous nature of technology in the United States. Studies indicate that neurological changes occur with continuous exposure to technology could account for some of the differences in cognitive achievement (Davidson, 2011; Kaku, 2016).

The novelty of the iPad at certain stages of the data collection may also have affected outcomes as well. When the iPads were initially introduced for educational purposes, exposure to the iPad had been limited. The introduction of the iPad into the educational setting was itself new. The school whose data is included in this study created a strategic plan aimed at finding new ways to successfully implement technology and to integrate it into the curriculum. As a result, the administration investigated the possibilities and eventually determined that a one-to-one iPad program would best fit the needs of both the students and the school. The school began with a roll-out of new iPads to teachers a year prior to introducing them to students. This did allow teachers time to gain some familiarity with the iPad before the students were provided with them.

In 2012, the iPad was introduced as an instructional tool in the classroom at the school whose data are included in this study. Over time, more specific professional development opportunities were made available. Methods of instruction did change as time progressed, and the educators did become more comfortable with the functions and features of the iPad. Eventually, exposure to the iPad and its multimodalities increased educator awareness and led to changes in instructional methods that were aimed at improving outcomes. It is my belief that because iPad instruction is still in its infancy stages, outcomes will continue to be positively affected if more research is conducted and methods of instruction are adjusted as a result of these findings.

Developers of new technologies could potentially make one of the biggest impacts on the use of iPad-based instruction in the classroom if they would simply acquiesce that the all-in-one nature of this technology is having a detrimental impact on educational outcomes when it is used a tool for learning. If the developers of new technologies are willing to implement changes, the iPad (or some other form of screen-based, mobile technology) could take center stage as a revolution in the field of education.

CHAPTER 12

WHERE DO WE GO FROM HERE?

IMPLICATIONS OF THE STUDY

The iPad began to be introduced in classrooms across the United States in 2010. Today, one in three schools uses some form of iPad instruction (Herold, 2014). The implications of this study could be far reaching and influence school systems in ways both direct and indirect.

Direct implications. Direct implications of this study apply to the class and school settings. These implications focus on impact on students, faculty, and administrators within a given system.

Implications at the classroom level. The implications of the results of this study are many. First, adolescent students in 21st century classrooms are now being taught in both linear and multidirectional fashions. Once students reach high school, it is assumed that they have already developed the skills to follow information in a step-by-step progression and then attach that information to prior knowledge before determining an outcome. Many elementary schools now integrate technology into the curriculum as early as kindergarten, and this means that students may not have fully developed the level of skill with linear processes

The Rise of the Human Digital Brain:
How Multidirectional Thinking is Changing the Way We Learn, pages 111–119.

as former generations did. This in turn may impact success in high school classrooms where teachers assume a level of mastery already exists.

Many high school teachers still assume that the students come to them with the ability to think in a linear fashion when in fact, many students may not yet have truly mastered this skill. Many of these students have been reading on screens for so long that they may tend to skim and scan for information, and they may never have effectively developed the skills necessary for critical thinking and analysis. Twenty-first century students are in many cases unable to follow a pattern to connect information and determine a reasonable outcome without being explicitly taught how to do so. Teachers need to be aware of the changes occurring and should make needed adjustments to classroom instruction to better fit the needs of 21st century students.

If early education programs focused more on teaching linear thinking skills before introducing technology, the students might later be able to use technology as a scaffold to supplement learning rather than seeing it as a singular means of gathering information. Currently, the novelty of the iPad as a learning tool has led to students as young as age four being taught literacy skills first through the use of the iPad. This reinforces the surface-level reading skills necessary for decoding, but it does not reinforce the type of deep-level reading skills necessary for vocabulary acquisition and comprehension. It would be helpful to develop policies to determine when iPads should be first introduced and how they should be used to best support instruction in the classroom.

Implications at the school level. School administrators should be aware of the changing patterns of thought in 21st century students. As a result, they should support the creation of curriculum aimed at reinforcing the type of linear thought processes that encourage deeper analysis. Administrators should also support the creation of curriculum aimed at enhancing the type of multidirectional thinking that reinforces and supports student creativity. Since multidirectional thinking is synonymous with nonlinear thinking, it is characterized by expansion in many directions, and there are multiple places from which one may apply logic. Professional development opportunities (PDs) should be designed to educate teachers about the neurological changes occurring in modern students and these PD's should encourage teachers to support new forms of learning. These new forms of learning should support both linear and nonlinear reading strategies, and these strategies should be introduced at the appropriate age and stage in cognitive development.

Digital literacies should also be incorporated into curriculum standards. Digital literacies are defined as "the assortment of cognitive-thinking strategies that consumers of digital information utilize" (Osterman, 2012, p. 135). As research indicates, very few standards currently pertain to digital literacies, yet digital literacy is necessary for success in 21st century classrooms (James, 2015; Leu et al., 2011). To more effectively teach important 21st century skills, digital literacies should be taught in schools in such a way that children are consistently exposed to them. This will reinforce the type of cognitive strategies necessary for effective use of technology as a tool for learning.

Schools could also use this information to create literacy learning environments that are more hybrid in nature. This study includes results that may have occurred for multiple reasons. The small class setting provided to the students in this study may have had an impact on achievement. Small group learning could also have impacted the results. Extended time was another component of this program that may have had an impact on the results. The incorporation of a novel-of-choice program was another element that may have impacted the outcomes of the study. Using an iPad in conjunction with one or all of these components while developing a program that is more equitable in time distribution could possibly yield a higher effect size.

Indirect implications. There are many implications outside of the classroom and school that will impact the direction of education in the future. Some of the indirect implications affect software developers and education policy makers.

Implications for software developers. The functions of the iPad provide new and unprecedented access to information. Students today have the potential to become multidirectional thinkers who can make connections more quickly and accurately than ever before. If Apple and other developers of educationally specific technology create devices that are primarily designed as tools for education rather than as "catch-all" learning and entertainment devices, perhaps the educational potential of the devices could be fully realized. Apple has recently made attempts to help educators monitor student use of the iPad with the introduction of Apple Classroom, a recent update that allows an educator to see all the screens of students on his or her iPad. While intended to be helpful, this can also create a challenge.

Educators are busy attempting to deliver information to the whole group and splitting time between directly engaging students and monitoring a screen can be difficult. Once direct instruction is completed, educators often take time to work with individual students, and this is another time when it is difficult to focus on the primary task (the needs of the individual student) and the screen that requires monitoring. The entire onus is on the educator, and it is nearly impossible to successfully keep track of individual student iPad usage while attempting to effectively implement instruction that will achieve the desired growth. While Apple Classroom is good in theory, its practical applications are limited.

Apple also recently introduced a new feature called "guided access." This feature allows educators to set a code that will lock a student into a particular application until the teacher unlocks the student's device by reapplying the code. While this feature may be helpful when students are taking tests, it does not allow a student to use the full functions of the iPad while writing a paper or reading for information as that student cannot navigate to other sites when she has questions. Additionally, guided access must be applied to each iPad individually, and this can be time consuming and difficult to effectively implement. The potential of the iPad for remediation could be tremendous, but only if the technology is improved to remove unwanted distractions when devices are being used in educational settings for educational purposes.

Implications at the policy level. Current educational policies do not always incorporate digital literacies. Digital citizenship, which is defined as "the norm of appropriate, responsible technology use" (Davidson, 2011, p. 17), is one area that should be incorporated into policy as well as into professional development. Areas affected by digital citizenship include digital access, digital commerce, digital communication, digital literacy, digital etiquette, digital law, digital rights and responsibilities, digital health and wellness, and digital security (Davidson, 2011). With the many areas that digital citizenship encompasses, policies must be created to reflect each of them. These policies will impact literacy skills because once students become more aware of the impact of inappropriate use of digital media on their educations and on their lives, the hope is that they will add to their existing schemas and develop better decision making skills.

Education programs at universities could use the results of the analysis of data in this study to create policies aimed at increasing awareness among educators of the neurological changes occurring in 21st century students. These policies could change the way that education programs across the United States are structured. The more rigid method of instruction in education programs could give way to more creative and innovative offerings. Potential educators could benefit from training aimed at teaching students how to use deep-learning strategies before introducing them to the surface-learning strategies of the iPad.

Policies regarding educating students with diagnosed learning disabilities should also be reconsidered. The use of extended time and preferential seating are standard accommodations. Policies should begin to reflect the addition of new technologies available that can help to mitigate specific learning differences. The iPad can be used to record lectures for students with reading disorders or disorders of written expression. It may also be used to write a paper using the voice-to-text feature for a student with a disorder of written expression. There are also new type styles, such as OpenDyslexic, that can easily be downloaded onto the iPad to help students with reading disorders to understand class notes with greater clarity. Access to Learning Ally, a digital library of more than 80,000 narrator read books, is also easily available to dyslexic students via the iPad. All these features allow for greater differentiation and may unlock the abilities of students who previously had no medium available to them through which to demonstrate their true cognitive abilities. If school policies begin to add additional accommodations for students with diagnosed learning disabilities, these students may also be able to demonstrate greater achievement on assessments.

COGNITIVE TRAINING

A 2017 study entitled *LearnRx Cognitive Training for Children and Adolescents ages 5–18: Effects on Academic Skills, Behavior, and Cognition,* had some interesting results. Cognitive training is trainer-delivered and occurs during 60–90-minute training sessions that happens 3–4 hours a week. This is a 60-hour model from the start of the program to finish. A "drill for skill" method is used to help individuals master certain skills. The trainers use adaptive levels of intensity, hierarchical sequencing, task loading, and dynamic feedback to move the participants through the curriculum. Deliberate distractions are also added to tax the participant's attention and focus skills. One task example is a "memory match," which is developed to target working memory, visual discrimination, processing speed, visual span, and sustained attention. There are nine difficulty levels and 34 variations of training task. The pre- and post-test measures were in the form of a Woodcock-Johnson Test of Cognitive Abilities. It should be noted that psychologists are not conducting these tests when they are used as measures at Learning RX facilities and only certain portions of the test are utilized.

There were a series of additional measures (in conjunction with the Woodcock-Johnson) used in this study (both qualitative and quantitative) to determine effectiveness of the program. What I found most interesting about the results were the effect sizes. For long term memory, the effect size was 1.02, which would be equivalent to two to three years of growth over the course of 60 hours of training. Auditory processing had an effect size of 0.95, which again would equate to two to three years of growth. Working memory was not impacted as greatly with an effect size of 0.66, but this still equates to greater growth than would be obtained over the course of a school year. The greatest impact was in attention. This had an effect size of 1.21. This indicates that a student with ADHD who undergoes this training stands to benefit substantially from cognitive training.

The study also broke down the results to look at the differences between 5–12-year old participants and 13–18-year old participants. The 13–18-year old participants did benefit from cognitive training as it related to memory, processing speed, and attention, but the reading program showed no substantial gains for this age group. It did, however, produce gains in both reading and thinking abilities for 5–12-year old participants (Jedlinka, 2017). These results should be viewed with caution as they represent just one study, but they are interesting and indicate a need for future research in this area.

TOO MUCH TREBLE OR TOO MUCH BASS

As we attempt to integrate processes, it is much like using the knobs on the old stereo systems to achieve the perfect sound. You adjust the treble and then the bass and continue to slightly move each knob up or down until the perfect balance is found and the sound is what you want to achieve. This type of synthesis can occur in the educational process as well. The problem is that we have not yet mastered a way to achieve balance for each individual. We are used to attempting to set the balance for the whole group and expecting each individual to adjust as necessary to meet the group average.

According to Dr. Daniel Amen, a psychologist who uses brain imaging to help him understand individual needs, psychological treatment needs to be tailored to individual brains, and the technology exists to make this happen. Is this not also true about education? Amen has seen through brain imaging that it is possible to literally change people's brains if the right treatments are put in place (Amen, 2011). Wouldn't it be amazing if we applied this same knowledge to the field of education rather than developing plans based on group averages?

An analogy for this would be taking twenty stereos that were made by different manufacturers and placing them together in one room. One individual enters the room and adjusts the treble and bass for one of the stereos. Once the perfect balance has been found, the individual then proceeds to go to each of the other stereos and use the same settings rather than realizing that the other stereos may require different adjustments due to the differences in their internal components. While the results may come close to meeting needs, the adjustments may be way off for some of the units.

This is similar to what happens in many classrooms today. We teach to the average and do not adjust for differences (other than providing accommodations such as extended time and preferential seating for students with diagnosed learning disabilities). If we simply realize that each individual may require different accommodations (or settings), perhaps we can move away from the model of using group averages to determine best practices for individual students.

A NONLINEAR MIND FORCED INTO A LINEAR MOLD

Since school is designed to reinforce linear processes, what happens to a nonlinear mind forced into a linear mold? A good way to better understand the nonlinear, multi-directional thinker is to reflect back to Plato's *Allegory of the Cave.* In this allegory, Plato envisions a cave where a group of individuals sits staring at shadows on one wall of the cave. The only reality that the individuals know is what they see projected on that one wall. They cannot look to the left or the right, and they have no idea who is behind them projecting those shadows. In the case of the 20th century classroom (which has extended into the 21st century), the teacher would be the one projecting the shadows on the wall. The difference is that now the students have the ability to look left and right and behind themselves, and they are aware that the teacher is the one projecting the shadows. They can access information from other resources to either prove or disprove what the educator is presenting and are, therefore, possibly more enlightened than previous groups who also occupied the cave.

In *The Allegory of the Cave*, there is only one enlightened individual who is aware of the individuals behind the group projecting the shadows. When he tries to make the rest of the group aware of what is occurring, they become afraid and kill the enlightened one. In the 21st century, technology has created an entire group of enlightened ones who now know more about the world and what is happening in it than any previous generations in history. As a result, they are demanding answers from those casting the shadows. This makes those casting the shadows uncomfortable, and it causes them to question their position as the keepers of the knowledge. In a nutshell, that is why change is so difficult to achieve. The generation teaching this new group of nonlinear thinkers was indoctrinated in a system that reinforced linear thinking. The educators still believe they are the "sage on the stage," and this prevents them from allowing themselves to become the "guide on the side."

The "shadow casters" must now assume a new identity to be successful. They must become "clarifiers." They must help this new generation to clarify questions, to discern truth from lies, and to truly analyze and synthesize information in a way that will help all of us to succeed. Much of this will depend upon the early reinforcement of linear processes, but it will also need to tap into the new dawning of creativity that may emerge from this multidirectional design.

According to futurist Alvin Toffler, we need to add a new literacy skill to the three R's of reading, writing, and arithmetic, and that skill is the ability to learn, unlearn, and relearn (Davidson 2011 p. 19). To do this effectively, we must understand our present patterns and then learn how to break those patterns that are no longer useful. This is what most of us are not willing to do. We cling to the familiar and fight to hold onto what we believe to be the "correct way" to do things. What if our students really are the "enlightened ones" and we are now the ones unable to see what is happening around us? Are we attempting to destroy our students' creativity so that we can maintain a pattern that we feel most comfortable with?

Many teachers will tell you that students must learn in these predictable linear patterns because the systems in the world that we live in are primarily linear. That may be true in that the current man-made systems do follow these linear patterns, but what about the future? According to information cited by Cathy Davidson in her book *Now You See it: How the Brain Science of Attention Will Transform the Way We Live, Work, and Learn*, "Sixty-five percent of children entering grade school this year will end up working in careers that haven't even been invented yet" (p. 18). Additionally, most systems in nature do not follow linear patterns. As we move further away from linear processes, perhaps we are moving closer towards processes that are more self-sustaining and viable.

HOW DO WE ACHIEVE BALANCE IN 21ST CENTURY CLASSROOMS?

It appears that the answer to the problems in education today are many, and there is no one easy answer. However, if we seek to achieve balance, we may be able to make the first strides in helping the next generation to enjoy the educational process and to become independent thinkers. If we fail to realize that balance is essential, we risk creating a generation that is distracted, uncertain, and lost in all the information that they have access to but have no idea what to do with.

We must strike a balance between linear processes and technology. Students would benefit from being taught linear processes early on without the interruption of technology. Dr. Michael Gurian suggests that a child should not even be presented with an iPhone until they are at least 14 years old. This is because modern neuroscience informs us that the changes that are occurring in the brains of children who are constantly exposed to technology are working against their ability to understand the knowledge that they are accessing.

Additionally, we have tech companies who have tapped into these changes and are using this information for profit. These companies understand, by reviewing neuroscience, how to make children, particularly boys, addicted to certain forms of technology. We know that from infancy, most boys' brains are wired to attempt something as many times as necessary to achieve success. The games available to them via the iPad, which is also used in many schools for educational purposes, are tapping into the spatial-visual and mechanical reasoning of boys and using this to make money. Because iPads are "catch all" devices used for both entertainment and education, it is difficult for children to separate the two. Boys, who stand to benefit tremendously from the multimodalities available via the iPad, are being distracted by games and other social features of the iPad and, as a result, they are unable to tap into its full potential as an educational platform. One answer to today's educational woes would be to create a technological platform that is designed purely for educational purposes.

A SUCCESSFUL MODEL FOR 21ST CENTURY LEARNING

We must remember that nonlinear thinkers cannot connect the dots unless they are first taught how to think in linear patterns. They must see how math is connected to science and how language is connected to history. One way to create a viable model that would reinforce both linear and multidirectional thinking would be to break the school day up into two parts. The first part of the day would concentrate on presenting important "background" information. Concepts in math, science, history, and English would be taught and analyzed during this time. Each student would be encouraged to see connections between the subjects. For example, history lessons would mirror time periods being discussed in literature classes. Students would be asked to see, understand, and make specific connections. How did the events in history influence this literature? How was this literature used to reinforce certain norms in society during that time period? How was it used to subjugate certain populations?

The afternoon would be comprised of break-out sessions where students would be encouraged to work on projects of passion. If a student is passionate about cars, he would be encouraged to take courses in engineering to help him understand the complexities of the systems necessary to create a vehicle. He would connect the math and science that he learned earlier, and even the history and literature, to help him envision new modes of transportation. He would spend the afternoon synthesizing the information that he learned in the morning. Pathways to success would no longer be one-dimensional and measured on a single scale. Competitions could be created between students to see who could envision the most effective and efficient form of travel for the 21st century. This type of learning would no longer be rote, and it could indeed transform not only our educational system, but it could transform the world in which we live.

FINAL THOUGHTS

According to the Partnership for 21st Century Learning (P21), there are four C's that we must keep in mind as we develop education for 21st century students: critical thinking, communication, creativity, and collaboration. As students become adults and move into the workplace, we can narrow this down even further to two critical skills that will be necessary in the 21st century workplace: the ability to think and the ability to communicate.

We must come to a point in human history where we understand the value of both skills. Thinking is a process that requires an intricate series of connections to be made in the mind. Whether these connections are linear or not, they must be made before true understanding can take place. Once we develop our thinking and reasoning skills adequately, we must learn to communicate our ideas effectively with one another. Unfortunately, the art of communication seems to be what is getting lost in today's world of electronic devices. The most important skills necessary for success in the 21st century will center around our ability to understand and interpret the information in front of us and then to collaborate on ways to use this information most effectively for the good of human kind.

I was recently given the opportunity to attend the YMCA's Kentucky Youth Assembly, a noteworthy program that provides students interested in politics and community engagement an opportunity to come together and debate legislation created by other students from across the state. I was encouraged to see that over 20% of the bills written by these high school students for debate centered on the future of education. Our young people see the need for reform, and they are willing to be a part of the process. If we encourage them to use their talents and their voices to help reform our system of education, they may just take a moment to look up from their iPhones and engage in productive communication that will lead to positive outcomes.

According to Dr. Amen, "You can literally change people's brain, and when you do, you change their lives," (Amen, 2011). Since we have now identified that technology is changing our brains, we must also be willing to acknowledge that our lives will also change. Whether these changes will be negative or positive remains to be seen. What we can say with certainty, however, is that we have the potential to direct that change in any way that we choose. What we cannot afford to do is to sit by and do nothing while we wait to see where the change may take us.

GLOSSARY

Analytic Phonics—A more accelerated form of phonics where children are taught to recognize whole words by sight and later to break the word into smaller units of sound (Johnston, Logan, & Watson, 2009, p. 176).

App—An "app" or "application" is a software program, often designed to run on a mobile device, that allows the user to carry out one or more operations. Apps can be narrow or broad, simple or grand, and in either case are tightly controlled by the individual organization that designed the app (Gardner & Davis, 2013, p. 6).

Automaticity—The ability to do things without having to think about them at a conscious level. It occurs in virtually all overlearned behaviors. Automaticity is essential not only for effective reading, but also for effective learning (Tzelgov, 1999, p. 3).

Brain-Based Learning (BBL)—Brain-based learning involves accepting the rules of how the brain processes, and then organizing instruction bearing these results in mind to achieve meaningful learning (Caine & Caine, 1994, as cited in Duman, 2010, p. 2080).

Closed High School Placement Test (HSPT)—The Closed HSPT provides national normative measures in the cognitive and basic skills areas of verbal, qualitative, reading, mathematics, and language. This assessment mirrors the Scholas-

The Rise of the Human Digital Brain:
How Multidirectional Thinking is Changing the Way We Learn, pages 121–127.

tic Achievement Test (SAT) in that standard scores on each section of the HSPT range from 200 to 800, with 500 being the average score. Schools also receive a Cognitive Skills Quotient (CSQ). The CSQ measures the aptitude of the student for future learning on a scale from 55 to 145 with a means score of 100 (Scholastic Testing Services, Inc., 2009).

Cognitive Disequilibrium—When a child's existing schemas are not capable of explaining what it can perceive around it (Piaget, 1962, as cited in Burnett, 2010, p. 145).

Cognitive Equilibrium—When a child's existing schemas are capable of explaining what it can perceive around it, it is said to be in a state of equilibrium, i.e. a state of cognitive balance (Piaget, 1962, as cited in Burnett, 2010 p. 145).

Cognition—A term that refers to the mental functions such as thinking, remembering, and problem solving of the individual (James, 2015, p. 5).

Constrained Reading Skills—Skills that have boundaries or limits. There are 44 phonemes in English and 26 letters. As well, there are a finite number of letter combinations that represent sounds. And there is a limit as to the rate of reading one can sustain without sacrificing accuracy and meaning. These first four reading skills–phonemic awareness, alphabetics, phonics, and fluency–are constrained reading skills because we can count them, and they are easily measured (Fisher, Frey, & Hattie, 2016, p. 45).

Deep-Level Reading Strategies—Strategies that cause readers to engage with the text in a meaningful way. Some of these strategies include visualization, note taking, paraphrasing, underlining and discussing reading with others (Cantrell & Carter, 2009, p. 201).

Descriptive Statistics—Descriptive statistics can be described as statistical procedures that organize and summarize data (Cronk, 2012, p. 131).

Digital Citizenship—Norm of appropriate, responsible technology use (Davidson, 2011, p. 17).

Digital Literacy—The assortment of cognitive-thinking strategies that consumers of digital information utilize (Osterman, 2012, p. 135).

Direct Instruction—The explicit teaching of a skill-set using lectures or demonstrations of the material to students (Fisher et al., 2016, p. 7).

Dyslexia—Dyslexia is a recognized disability that interferes with the processes entailed in decoding, such as differentiation of phonemes, but not the higher-order cognitive processes involved in reading, such as drawing inferences from text (Koretz, 2008, p. 296).

Electronic Books (eBooks)—The electronic counterpart of a printed book, which can be viewed on a desktop computer, laptop, smartphone, tablet, or eBook reader (Borchers, 1999, p. 2).

Effect Size—'Effect size" (Cohen's *d*) is a way of quantifying the size of the difference between two groups. It is easy to calculate, readily understood, and can be applied to any measured outcome in Education or Social Science. It is particularly valuable for quantifying the effectiveness of a particular intervention, relative to some comparison. It allows us to move beyond the simplistic, "Does it work or not?" to the far more sophisticated, "How well does it work in a range of contexts?" Moreover, it places emphasis on the most important aspect of an intervention—the size of the effect—rather than its statistical significance (Coe, 2002, p. 1).

Extended Literacy Learning Opportunities—Providing multiple means of representation, action, expression, and engagement with adaptations to presentation formats provided during classroom instructional time as well as during additional time (in the case of this study, 50% more time) to introduce these learning opportunities to students (Bulgren, Graner, & Deschler, 2013, p. 18).

Independent-Samples *t*-Test—A test conducted to compare the means of two samples that are independent samples that were not from randomly assigned groups. Samples are independent if there is no relationship between them (Cronk, 2012, p. 11).

Information Age—The Information Age is the fastest and most global of all the four great epochs in the history of human communications. The Information Age is considered one of the greatest transformations in human interaction in history and is responsible for enormous changes in our modes of social interactions and communication (Davidson, 2011, p. 11).

Intensive Intervention—A process involving adaptation of a secondary intervention (Tier 2), that is more frequently and concretely quantitative rather than qualitative (National Center on Intensive Intervention, 2013, p. 31),

iPad—The iPad is a tablet computer developed by Apple. It is smaller than a typical laptop but significantly larger than the average smartphone. The iPad does not include a keyboard, but instead it has a touch screen interface that is used to control the device. Like the iPhone, the iPad runs Apple's iOS operating system. This allows the iPad to run third-party apps, which can be downloaded from Apple's App Store. Versions of the iPad include Wi-Fi capability, which can be used for surfing the Web, checking email, and downloading apps directly to the device (Christensson, 2011).

Learning Disability—According to the Individuals with Disabilities Education Act (IDEA), a specific learning disability is a disorder in one or more of the basic psychological processes involved in understanding or in using language, spoken or written, in which the disorder may manifest itself in the imperfect ability to listen, think, speak, read, write, spell, or do mathematical calculations (James 2015, p. 87).

Learning Processes—The interconnections between perception, memory, language, imagery, emotion, and motivation that allow students to mentally build connections between verbal and pictorial information patterns or between new and prior memories and integrate them with knowledge structures in the long-term memory" (Kuldas et al., 2013, p. 2).

Learning Styles—Cognitive, affective, and physiological traits that serve as relatively stable indicators of how learners perceive, interact with, and respond to the learning environment (O'Keefe & Nadal, 1978 as cited in Duman, 2010, p. 2079).

Linear Thinking—A process of thought following known cycles or step-by-step progression in which a response to a step must be elicited before another step is taken (Davidson, 2011, p. 15).

Low-achieving Readers—Older children with poor reading progress, varying in intelligence, at least some of whom achieved poorly in other academic areas (National Reading Panel, 2000, p. 90).

Meta-analysis—A method designed to increase the reliability of research by combining and analyzing the results of all known trials (Lenhard, 2013, p. 224).

Multidirectional Literacy—This term refers to the act of reading from a webpage and the point at which a reader first looks on the screen and the direction in which this might lead the reader (Rowsell & Burke, 2009, p. 107).

Multimodal—This term refers to the use of different modes of communication (such as sight, sound, touch, movement) to create an effect, the point being that each mode offers certain potential meanings that another may not offer (Rowsell & Burke, 2009, p. 107).

Multimodality Theory—Multimodality is a theory that looks at the many different modes that people use to communicate with each other and to express themselves. This theory is relevant as an increase in technology tools, and associated access to multimedia composing software, has led to people being able to easily use many modes in art, writing, music, and dance and every day interactions with each other (Kresse, 2009, p. 38).

Newsela—Newsela is a web-based interactive and adaptive current-events news site. Over time, Newsela creates customized reading levels for each student. The appropriate reading (or Lexile) level is set as students start reading and taking quizzes. Their progress provides feedback to Newsela on how well they understand what they read. Based on this information, Newsela adjusts the reading level for the individual students. Newsela tracks each student's progress and informs the teacher which students are on track, which students are behind, and which students are ahead (Davis, 2016, support.newsela.com).

Nelson-Denny Reading Test (NDRT) –This test is a trustworthy assessment of student ability in the areas of the related and interdependent skills of vocabulary and reading comprehension. It is composed of two subtests, vocabulary and comprehension. The vocabulary section consists of 80 items, each with five answer choices. The comprehension section consists of seven reading passages with a total of 38 questions, each with five answer choices (Brown, Fishco, & Hanna, 1993, p. 1).

Non-linear Thinking—Human thought characterized by expansion in many directions, rather than in one direction based on the concept that there are multiple places from which one can apply logic to a problem (Davidson, 2011, p. 16).

Unconstrained Reading Skills—Skills such as vocabulary and comprehension that have no endpoint (Fisher et al., 2016, p. 45).

Paired-Samples *t*-Test—A test used to determine if the means of two samples that come from the same population are statistically different from each other (Cronk, 2012, p. 12).

Prosody—Intonation, pacing, and expressiveness while reading aloud (Fisher et al., 2016, p. 63).

Quasi-Experimental Non-Equivalent Control Group Design—A research design method where comparison groups are not randomized, contain a pre-treatment and post-treatment measure, have a treated and untreated group, and are measured using an analysis of covariance using a post-test minus pre-test measure to evaluate the effect of the treatment being introduced (Cronk, 2012, p. 12).

Reading—Reading is the ability to decode and infer the meaning of printed text as commonly presented (Koretz, 2008, p. 296).

Reading Comprehension—Application and integration of strategies to sustain and regain meaning over longer pieces of text (Fisher et al., 2016, p. 16).

Reading Paths—This term plays a central role in multimodality theory. A reading path charts a reader's trajectory through a text, and it exists as much with printed texts as it does with digital texts (Rowsell & Burke, 2009, p. 107).

Repeated Reading—A method of instruction in which a student listens to a passage as it is read by a teacher and then reads the same passage to himself or herself before finally reading it aloud. Rate, accuracy, and prosody are calculated and reported to the students with the goal being an increase in all three with subsequent attempts (Fisher, et al., 2016, p. 63).

Response to Intervention (RTI)—The components of a response to intervention effort include universal screening, quality core instruction, progress monitoring, and supplemental and intensive interventions (Fisher et al., 2016, p. 143).

Schema—A cohesive repeatable action sequence possessing component actions that are tightly interconnected and governed by a core meaning (Piaget, 1952, p. 12).

Significance Level—The significance level (often referred to as the rejection level) is often set at .05 or .01. When a difference is statistically significant at .05 level, a difference that large occurs less than 5% of the time if the null were true (Howell, 2013, p. 94).

Surface-Level Reading Strategies—Strategies that involve initial access to text comprehension such as adjusting reading speed, omitting unknown words, and re-reading (Cantrell & Carter, 2009, p. 201).

Synthetic Phonics—This is a form of reading instruction in which the sounds of letters are used in smaller units and then are put together with (or synthesized with) other letters and sounds (Johnston, et al., 2009, p. 176).

Tablet—A tablet, or tablet PC, is a portable computer that uses a touch-screen as its primary input device. Most tablets are slightly smaller and weigh less than the average laptop (Christensson, 2011).

Transformative Learning—Transformative learning is a learning process that begins with learners' experiences. The learner must critically self-examine the assumptions and beliefs that have structured how the experience has been interpreted. This sets in motion a revision of specific assumptions about oneself and others until every structure of assumption has been transformed (Merriam, Caffarella, & Baumgartner, 2007, p. 185).

Universal Design—Universal design refers to three principles of planning instruction: providing multiple means of representation, providing multiple means of action and expression, providing multiple means of engagement (McMahon, 2014, p. 39).

Vocabulary—The denotative and connotative meanings of words and phrases (Fisher et al., 2016, p. 45).

Web-based Interactive Technology—This form of technology includes any form of interactive technology accessed v+ia the World Wide Web with a focus on providing multimodal learning opportunities for students (Rowsell & Burke, 2009, p. 107).

REFERENCES

Amen, D. (2011 June), *Change your brain, change your life.* (Video file). Retrieved from https://www.youtube.com/watch?v=MLKj1puoWCg

Americans with Disabilities Act of 1990, Pub. L. No. 101–336, § 12102, 104 Stat. 328 (1990).

Berman, D. (2003). Technology has us so plugged into data, we turned off. *Wall Street Journal—Eastern Edition, 242*(93), B1–B1.

Borchers, J. (1999). *Electronic books: Definitions, genres, interaction design patterns.* (pp. 1–8). Linz, Austria: Linz University. Retrieved from http://www.hci-twth-aachen.de

Bradbury, R. (1953). *Farhenheit 451.* New York, NY: Ballentine Books.

Brady, L. (1995). *Curriculum development, 5th edition.* Sydney, Australia: Prentice-Hall.

Brown, J. I., Fishco, V., & Hanna, G. (1993). *Nelson-Denny reading test: Manual for scoring and interpretation.* Rolling Meadows, IL: Riverside Publishing Company.

Bulgren J., Graner, P., & Deschler, D. (2013). Literacy challenges and opportunities for students with learning disabilities in social studies and history. *Learning Disabilities Research & Practice, 28*(1), 17–27.

Burnett, S. (2010). Substantiating constructivism from a brain-based perspective. *The International Journal of Interdisciplinary Social Sciences, 5*(4), 145–152.

Caine, R. N., & Caine, G. (1994). *Making connections: Teaching and the human brain.* New York, NY: Addison-Wesley.

Cantrell, S. & Carter, J. (2009). Relationships among learner characteristics and Adolescents' perceptions about reading strategy use. *Reading Psychology, 30*(3), 195–224.

The Rise of the Human Digital Brain:
How Multidirectional Thinking is Changing the Way We Learn, pages 129–135.

Cheung, A., & Slavin, R. (2014). Effects of educational technology applications on reading outcomes for struggling readers: A best-evidence synthesis. *Reading Research Quarterly, 48*(3), 277–299.

Christensson, P. (2011, March 9). *iPad definition.* Retrieved 2016, July 29, from http://techterms.com.

Coe, Robert (2002, September). *It's the effect size, stupid: What effect size is and why it is important.* Paper presented at the British Education Research Association Annual Conference, Exeter, England.

Coles, M., & Hall, C. (2002). Gendered readings: Learning from children's reading choices. *Journal of Research in Reading, 25*(1), 96–108.

Common Core State Standards Initiative (2010, June). *Common core state standards for English language arts & literacy in history/social studies, science, and technical subjects.*

Conway, P. F., & Amberson, J. (2011). Laptops meet schools, one-one draw: M-learning for secondary students with literacy difficulties. *Support for Learning, 26*(4), 173–181.

Coulson, A. (2017). The price of excellence (PBS series episode one). *A personal journey with Andrew Coulson.* PBS. Retrieved from http://www.pbs.org/whet/school.inc

Cronk, B. (2012). *How to use SPSS,* (7th ed.). Glendale, CA: Pyrzcak Publishing.

Davidson, C. (2011). *Now you see it: How the brain science of attention will transform the way we live, work and learn.* New York, NY: Viking Press.

Davis, N. (2016, 2 June). How Newsela determines a student's reading level. *Newsela Support.* Support.newsela.com.

Doidge, N. (2007). *The brain that changes itself: Stories of personal triumph from the frontiers of brain science.* New York, NY: Penguin Books.

Duman, B. (2010). The effects of brain-based learning on the academic achievement of Students with different learning styles. *Educational Sciences: Theory and Practice, 10*(4), 2078–2099.

Eagleman, D. (2015). *The brain: The story of you.* New York, NY: Vintage Books.

Education Trust. (2017). *XQ Super school website. American-high school: Who succeeds and why.* Retrieved from: https://xqsuperschool.org/resources/infographics/who-succeeds-and-why

Feeney, N. (2015, 7 October). Women are now more likely to have a college degree than men. *Time Magazine.* http://time.com/4064665/women-college-degree/

Fisher, D., Frey, N., & Hattie, J. (2016). *Visible learning for literacy, grades K–12.* Thousand Oaks, CA: Sage Publishing Company.

Fraenkel, J., Wallen, N., & Hyun, H. (2012). *How to design and evaluate research in education.* (8th ed.). New York, NY: McGraw-Hill Publishing.

Friedman, T., (2016). *Thank you for being late: An optimist's guide to thriving in the age of acceleration.* New York, NY: Farar, Strauss, and Giroux.

Gardner, H., & Davis, K. (2013). *The app generation: How today's youth navigate identity, intimacy, and imagination in a digital world.* New Haven, CT: Yale University Press.

Goldstein, M., & Otte, G. (2016). *Change we must: Deciding the future of higher education.* New York, NY: Rosetta Books.

Graves, M. F. (1986). Vocabulary learning and instruction. *Review of educational research, 13*(2), 49–89.

Gurian, M. (2017a, June). *Boys and girls learn differently: Why gender-based instruction works.* Presented at the National Conference on Innovative Teaching Strategies, Las Vegas, NV.

Gurian, M. (2017b). *Saving our sons: A new path for raising healthy, resilient boys.* Spokane, WA: Gurian Institute Press.

Gurian, M., & Stevens, K. (2007). *The minds of boys: Saving our sons from falling behind in school and life.* San Francisco, CA: Josey Bass.

Greenfield, S. (2008). *ID: The quest for meaning in the 21st century.* London, England: Holden and Stoughton Ltd.

Harris, T. (2016, June 1). *Tristan Harris: How better tech could protect us from distractions* (Video file). Retrieved from https://www.ted.com/speakers/tristan_harris

Hattie, J. (2009). *Visible learning: A synthesis of over 800 meta-analyses relating to achievement.* New York, NY: Routledge.

Hattie, J. (2012). *Visible learning for teachers: Maximizing impact on learning.* New York, NY: Routledge.

Henderson, L. L., Weighall, A., & Gaskell, G. (2013). Learning new vocabulary during childhood: Effects of semantic training on lexical consolidation and integration. *Journal of Experimental Child Psychology, 116*(3), 572–592.

Hernandez, D., (April 10, 2017). How I learned to take the ACT like a rich kid. *The New York Times.* Retrieved from: https://www.nytimes.com/2017/04/10/opinion/how-i-learned-to-take-the-sat-like-a-rich-kid.html

Herold, B. (2014). Digital reading poses learning challenges for students. *Education Digest, 80*(1), 44–48.

Hoffman, C. (11 May, 2014). PCs before windows: What Using MS-DOS was actually like. *How to Geek.* Retrieved from: https://www.howtogeek.com/188980/pcs-before-windows-what-using-ms-dos-was-actually-like/

Hough, L. (2015). Beyond average. *Harvard Ed. Magazine* (Fall Edition), 15–16.

Howell, D. (2013). *Statistical methods for psychology* (8th ed). Belmont, CA: Wadsworth.

Individuals with Disabilities Education Act. (2004). 20 U.S.C. § 1400.

James, A. N., (2015). *Teaching the male brain: How boys think, feel, and learn in school* (2nd ed.). Thousand Oaks, CA: Corwin.

Jantz, G. L. (2014). Brain differences between genders. *Psychology Today.* Retrieved from: https://www.psychologytoday.com/blog/hope-relationships/201401/brain-differences-between-genders

Jaschik, S. (2016). ACT scores drop as more take test. *Inside Higher Ed.,* Retrieved from: https://www.insidehighered.com/news

Jedlicka, E. J. (2017, 27 November). LearningRx cognitive training for children and adolescents ages 5–18: Effects on academic skills, behavior and cognition. *Frontiers in Education 2*(62), 1–13.

Johnston, R. S., Logan, S., & Watson, J. E. (2009). Enhancing word reading, spelling and Reading comprehension skills with synthetic phonics teaching: Studies in Scotland and England. *Contemporary Perspectives on Reading and Spelling*, 131–145.

Kaku, M. (2014). *The future of the mind: The scientific quest to understand, enhance, and empower the mind.* New York, NY: Doubleday.

Kardaras, N. (2016). It's digital heroin': How screens turn kids into psychotic junkies. *New York Times.* Retrieved from http://nypost.com/2016/08/27/its-digital-heroin-how-screens-turn-kids-into-psychotic-junkies/1472626800/

Kervin, L., Verenikina, I., Jones, P., & Beath, O. (2013). Investigating synergies between literacy, technology, and classroom practice. *Australian Journal of Language & Literacy, 36*(3), 135–147.

Kittle, P. (2013). *Book love: Developing depth, stamina, and passion in adolescent readers.* Portsmouth, NH: Heinemann.

Koretz, D. (2008). *Measuring up: What educational testing really tells us.* Cambridge, MA: Harvard University Press.

Kresse, G. (2009). *Multimodality: A social semiotic approach to contemporary communication.* New York, NY. Routledge.

Kuhn, M. R., & Stahl, S. A. (2003). Fluency: A review of developmental and remedial practices. *Journal of Educational Psychology, 95*(3), 3–21.

Kuldas, S., Ismail, H. N., Hashim, S., & Bakar, Z. A. (2013). Unconscious learning processes: Mental integration of verbal and pictorial instructional materials. *Springer Plus, 2*(105), 1–63.

Larson, L. C. (2012). It's time to turn the digital page: Pre-service teachers explore e-Book reading. *Journal of Adolescent & Adult Literacy, 56*(4), 280–290.

Learning Disabilities Association of America (April 2001). *Reading and learning disabilities.* Retrieved from https://ldaamerica.org/advocacy/lda-position-papers/reading-and-learning-disabilities/

Lenhard, W. (2013). Rethinking strategy instruction: direct reading strategy instruction versus computer-based guided practice. *Journal of Research in Reading, 36*(2), 223–240.

Leu, D. J., McVerry, J., O'Byrne, W., Kiili, C., Zawilinski, L., Everett-Cacopardo, H., & Forzani, E. (2011). The new literacies of online reading comprehension: Expanding the literacy and learning curriculum. *Journal of Adolescent & Adult Literacy, 55*(1), 5–14.

Logan, S., & Johnston, R. S. (2009). Gender difference in reading ability and attitudes: Examining where these differences lie. *Journal of Research in Reading, 32*(2), 199–214.

Logan, S. & Johnston, R. S. (2010). Investigating gender differences in reading. *Educational Review, 62*(2), 175–187.

Martin, R. L. (2007, June), How successful leaders think. *Harvard Business Review.* Retrieved from: https://hbr.org/2007/06/how-successful-leaders-think.

Mayer, R. E., & Moreno, R. (2003). Nine ways to reduce cognitive load in multimedia learning. *Educational Psychology, 38*(1), 43–52.

McMahon, D. (2014). Universal design for learning features and tools on iPads and other iOS devices. *Journal of Special Education Technology*, 29(2), 39–49.

Meadows, D. (2008). *Thinking in systems: A primer.* White River Junction, VT: Chelsea Green Publishing.

Merzenich, M. (2004, February). *Merzenich, Michael: Growing evidence of brain plasticity* (Video file). Retrieved from https://www.ted.com/talks/michael_merzenich_on_the_elastic_brain

Merriam, S., Caffarella, R., & Baumgartner, L., (2007). *Learning in adulthood: A comprehensive guide* (3rd ed.). San Francisco, CA: Jossey-Bass.

MetaMetrics, (2009). *The Lexile framework for reading.* Retrieved 2016, October 7 from https://d1jt5u2s0h3gkt.cloudfront.net/m/cms_page_media/123/What-does-the-Lexile-measure-mean_1.pdf

Meyer, N., & Bouck, E. (2014). The impact of text-to-speech on expository reading for adolescents with LD. *Journal of Special Education, 29*(1), 21–31.

National Assessment of Educational Progress. (2005). *The nation's report card.* Retrieved from https://nces.ed.gov/nationsreportcard/pdf/studies/2005456.pdf

National Assessment of Educational Progress. (2012). *Trends in academic progress: Reading 1971–2012.* Retrieved from https://nces.ed.gov/nationsreportcard/subject/publications/main2012/pdf/2013456.pdf

National Center for Education Statistics. (2003). *The nation's report card: Reading, 2011.* Washington, DC; National Center for Education Sciences, U.S. Department of Education.

National Center for Educational Evaluation and Regional Assistance. (2003). *The enhanced reading opportunities study: Findings for the second year of implementation.* Retrieved from: http:ies.ed.gov/ncee/pubs/20094036/

National Center on Intensive Intervention. (2013). *Data-based individualization: A framework for intensive intervention.* (Publication No. H326Q110005). Retrieved from http://www.intensiveintervention.org/sites/default/files/DBI_Framework.pdf

National Reading Panel Report (2000). *Teaching Children to read: An Evidence-based assessment of the scientific research literature on reading and its implications for reading instruction.* (Publication No. 004769). Retrieved from https://www.nichd.nih.gov/publications/pubs/nrp/pages/smallbook.aspx

Nelson, L., Melina, A., Williams, N., & Sudweeks, A. (2014). Determining adolescent struggling readers' word attack skills with the core phonics survey. *Reading Improvement, 51*(4), 333–340.

Neuman, S. (2006). Speak up! *Early Childhood Today, 20*(4), 12–13.

Neuroplasticity (2017). *MedTerms Medical Dictionary A–Z* online. Retrieved February 8, 2017 from https://www.medicinenet.com/script/main/art.asp?articlekey=40362

O'Keefe, J., & Nadel, L. (1978). *The hippocampus as a cognitive map.* Oxford, UK: Clarendon Press.

Oppenheimer, T. (2003). *The flickering mind: Saving education from the false promise of technology.* New York, NY: Random House Trade Publications.

Osterman, M.D. (2012). Digital literacy: Definition, theoretical framework, and competencies. *Proceedings of the 11th Annual College of Education & GSN Research Conference,* (pp. 135–141). Miami: Florida International University. Retrieved from http://education.fiu.edu/research_conference/

Papert, S., & Harel, I. (1991). *Constructionism: Research reports and essays, 1985–1990.* Norwood, NJ: Ablex.

Park, J. (2012). A different kind of reading instruction: Using visualizing to bridge reading comprehension and critical literacy. *Journal of Adolescent and Adult Literacy, 55*(7) 629–640.

Paris, S. G. (2005). Reinterpreting the development of reading skills. *Reading Research Quarterly, 40*(2), 184–202.

Piaget, J. (1952). *The origins of intelligence in children.* New York, NY: International University Press, Inc.

Piaget, J. (1962). *Play, dreams and imitation in childhood.* New York, NY: W.W. Norton & Company, Inc.

Pinar, W., Reynolds, W. Slattery, P., and Taubman, P. (Eds.) (1995). *Understanding Curriculum.* New York, NY: Peter Lang.

Price, G. A. (2006). Creative solutions to making the technology work: Three case studies of dyslexic writers in higher education. ALT-J: *Research in Learning Technology, 14*(1), 21–38.

Rader, L. (2010). Teaching students to visualize: Nine key questions for success. *Preventing School Failure, 54*(2) 126–132.

Reichert, M., & Hawley, R. (2014). *I can learn from you: Boys as relational learners.* Boston, MA: Harvard Education Press.

Reid, G., Strnadová, I., & Cumming, T. (2013). Expanding horizons for students with Dyslexia in the 21st century: universal design and mobile technology. *Journal of Research in Special Educational Needs, 313*(3), 175–181.

Ritter, M. Caspi, A. Fergusson, D. M. Horwood, L. J., Goodman, R., & Maughan, B. (2004). Gender differences in reading difficulties: Findings from four epidemiology studies. *Journal of the American Medical Association,* 291, 2007–2012.

Rowsell, J. & Burke, A. (2009). Reading by design: Two case studies of digital reading practices. *Journal of Adolescent & Adult Literacy, 53*(2), 106–119.

Scholastic Testing Services Inc., (2009). High School Placement Test (HSTP). Retrieved from www.ststesting.com/hp_2.html

Selwyn, N., (2016). *Is technology good for education?* Malden, MA: Polity Press.

Senge, P., Cambron-McCabe, N., Lucas, T., Smith, B., et al. (2012). *Schools that learn: A fifth discipline fieldbook for educators, parents, and everyone who cares about education.* New York, NY: Crown Business.

Shaywitz, S. E. (2003). *Overcoming dyslexia: A new and complete science-based program for reading problems at any level.* New York, NY: Alfred A. Knopf, Inc.

Strauss, V. (April 22, 2014). What Does the SAT measure? Aptitude? Achievement? Anything? *Washington Post News.* Retrieved from www.wastingtonpost.com/news/answer-sheet/wp/2014/04/22/what-does-the-sat-measure

Topping, K. J. (2006). Building reading fluency: Cognitive, behavioral, and socioemotional factors and the role of peer-mediated learning. *Report: What reading has to say about reading fluency instruction* (pp. 106–129). Newark, DE: International Reading Association.

Twenge, J. (2017, September). Have smartphones destroyed a generation? *The Atlantic,* September 2017 issue. Retrieved from: https://www.theatlantic.com/magazine/archive/2017/09/has-the-smartphone-destroyed-a-generation/534198/

Tzelgov, J. (1999). Automaticity and processing without awareness. *Psyche, 5*(3), 1–8.

Updike, C., & Thornburg, J. (1992). Reading skills and auditory processing ability in children with chronic otitis media in early childhood. *The Annals of Otology, Rhinology, and Laryngology, 101*(6), 530–537.

Ur-Rehman, A., & Bokhari, M. (2011). Effectiveness of brain-based learning theory at secondary level. *International Journal of Academic Research, 3*(4), 354–359.

U.S. Department of Justice Civil Rights Division Disability Rights Section. *ADA Requirements.* Retrieved December, 2017 from www.ada.gov.

Wagner, T. (2014). *The global achievement gap.* New York, NY: Basic Books.

Wexler, J., Vaughn, S., Edmonds, M., & Reutebuch, C. K. (2008). A synthesis of fluency interventions for struggling secondary struggling readers. *Reading and Writing: An Interdisciplinary Journal, 21,* 317–347.

Wexler, J., Vaughn, S., Roberts, G., & Denton, C.A. (2010). The efficacy of repeated reading and wide reading practice for high school students with severe reading disabilities. *Learning Disabilities Research & Practice: A Publication for the Division of Learning Disabilities, Council for Exceptional Children, 25*(1), 2–10.

Wolf, M. (2010). Our deep reading brain: Its digital evolution poses questions. *Nieman Reports, 64*(2), 7.

Wolf, M., & Barzillai, M., (2009). The importance of deep reading. *Educational Leadership, 66*(6), 32–37.

Wujec, T. (2009, February). *Tom Wujec: Three ways the brain creates meaning* (video file). Retrieved from https://www.ted.com/talks/tom_wujec_on_3_ways_the_brain_creates_meaning

Wright, S., Fugett, A., & Caputa, F. (2013). Using E-readers and internet resources to support comprehension. *Journal of Educational Technology & Society, 16*(1), 367–379.

Yeatman, J., Dougherty, R., Ben-Shachar, M., & Wandell, B. (2012). Development of white matter and reading skills. *Proceedings of the National Academy of Sciences of the United States of America 109*(44), 17756–17757.

INDEX

The Rise of the Human Digital Brain:
How Multidirectional Thinking is Changing the Way We Learn, pages 137–139.

AUTHOR/EDITOR BIO

Dr. Beatriz Pacheco has worked in the field of education for 27 years as an English instructor, a reading teacher, a reading specialist, and a learning differences coordinator. Her experience includes work at the grade school, middle school, high school, and college levels. She has worked for public, private, and Department of Defense schools in North Carolina, New Mexico, Texas, Oklahoma, and Kentucky. Dr. Pacheco has also taught English courses for soldiers in the U.S. Army in Germany and South Korea. She currently works as a learning differences coordinator at a college-preparatory high school that launched a one-to-one iPad initiative in 2012, and the results of her study regarding the impact of iPad multimodalities on the vocabulary and comprehension of struggling adolescent readers are presented in her book *The Rise of the Human Digital Brain: How Multidirectional Thinking is Changing the Way We Learn.* Dr. Pacheco received her Doctorate in Educational Leadership in Louisville, Kentucky, and was the 2017 recipient of the Dr. Mary Angela Shaughnessy, SCN, Leadership Education Award from Spalding University for her contributions to educational research and for her leadership in the field of education.

The Rise of the Human Digital Brain:
How Multidirectional Thinking is Changing the Way We Learn, page 141.

CPSIA information can be obtained
at www.ICGtesting.com
Printed in the USA
BVHW08s2223041018
529344BV00005B/33/P